the
Thinking
Girl's
Guide *to*
Drinking

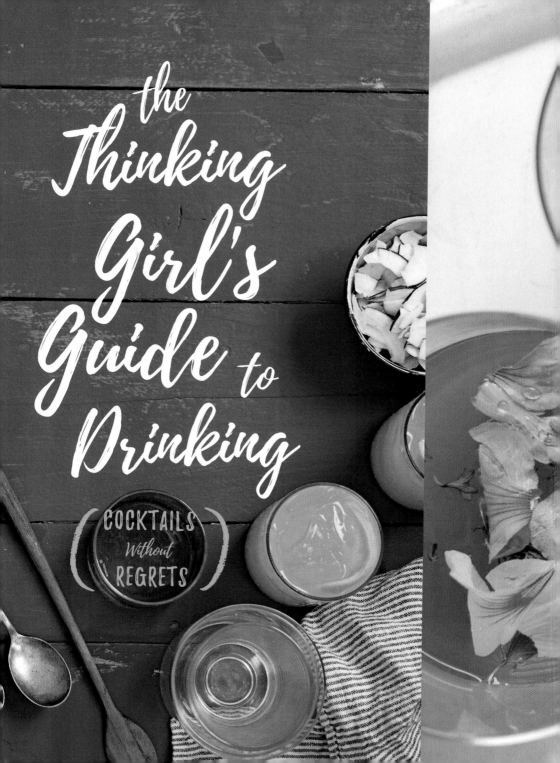

the Thinking Girl's Guide to Drinking

(COCKTAILS *Without* REGRETS)

ARIANE RESNICK, CNC

with

BRITTINI RAE

Food and Drink photography by Leela Cyd
Lifestyle photography by SMITHDAVIS

Regan Arts.
New York

Regan Arts.

65 Bleecker Street
New York, NY 10012

First Regan Arts paperback edition, November 2016

Library of Congress Control Number: 2016939714

ISBN 978-1-68245-048-2

Interior design by Laura Klynstra
Cover design by Richard Ljoenes
Drinks and food photography © Leela Cyd
Lifestyle photography © SMITHDAVIS

Printed in the United States

10 9 8 7 6 5 4 3 2 1

Dedicated to

Crystle, my twin flame,
and to all the thinking
girls out there

The connections we make in the course of
a life—maybe that's what heaven is.
—FRED ROGERS

Contents

Let's Think

If you want something to taste good, you probably ought to make it yourself; that's what my mom taught me, and it's what I have learned to be true throughout my life. My mother ran a co-op out of our basement, where wild rice in fifty-pound bags was scooped into portions for members and a ten-pound jar lived ubiquitously on a shelf in our finished basement. A friend in fifth grade asked me if the glass container was full of pencil tips—that's how ahead of the times we were.

For soda, my mom bought or made juice and mixed it with sparkling water. My dad kept twenty-five pounds of carrots in the spare fridge downstairs, which he juiced religiously in a Norwalk juicer and drank nightly for years. Thinking it revolutionary at the time, he now blames those thousands of glasses of fiberless sugar for his type 2 diabetes. He's controlled the diabetes for about twenty years now largely without medication.

I used that same methodology in my early thirties to heal my late-stage Lyme disease as well as the carbon monoxide poisoning I suffered a year after getting over the Lyme, fully recovering on my own and without pharmaceuticals. My family taught me to be empowered about my wellness, to be ahead of the curve on health trends, and to believe that the most delicious foods and drinks are the ones you make yourself. I took these lessons and applied them to every possible aspect of my life, and in turn, I am a healthy person who creates delicious meals and beverages. The fact that they gave me pots and pans and Tupperware to play with as a kid rather than commercial toys may also have had something to do with it.

I've been in and out of kitchens since my first job at age nineteen, when I was hired as the chef de cuisine of a vegetarian café in Gilroy, California—in part because of the unusual ability I had to make a chocolate cake out of chickpeas! In the mid-1990s, that wasn't yet common. Without any formal training, I composed buffet meals daily for fifty to one hundred guests and catered events for up to one hundred people at a time. The establishment didn't have an alcohol license, but I paired my meals with my homemade recipes for smoothies, juices, and tonics. It has been in my nature since I started this career to give people as full an experience as possible, taking care to match liquids and solids for the best dining delight. I had a wide assortment of jobs during those same years but always landed back in a kitchen, including a multiyear stint as the owner of a best-selling brand of raw vegan snacks. It was around this time that I realized the kitchen was probably where I belonged and finally learned to comfortably call myself a chef, something others had been calling me for years.

Because my life has involved a deep relationship with food and wellness, I've been all over the spectrum in terms of what I personally consume. At the intersection of vigilant health foodie and devil-may-care partyer, I found an amazing thing: happiness. I had spent most of my life following a restrictive healthy diet, spending many years on end without sugar, alcohol, caffeine, or grains on a low-carb quest for a level of perfection that I eventually realized was inhuman. It was also a whole lot of NO FUN. I took a break from that lifestyle in my late twenties and spent a few years partying hard. While it did have its moments, the end result was equal amounts of unpleasantness and lack of personal fulfillment.

Somewhere in my thirties, after the two major illnesses, I chilled out on pretty much every part of my life. I eased up on myself in regards to my diet, my weight, my career, my relationships—everything. In turn, things came together for me in a way they never had before. A relaxed attitude benefited me more than stringent guidelines ever had. I began operating through that relaxed perspective with nutrition and wellness clients, and found the emotional impact to be quite beneficial. Giving people permission to enjoy life is deeply healthful. While I began as a chef and certified nutritionist by helping others iron out diets relevant to their health issues, I slowly migrated into more of a coaching role, guiding others to make their own right choices in regards to everything from food to lifestyle. Somewhere along the way, I discovered that my purpose in life is simply to help others feel good, and that food and drink are the way I can help to do that. So here I've landed, in a place where, while I acknowledge that alcohol can have its downsides if not consumed responsibly, I've been able to incorporate it consciously and successfully into a healthy lifestyle, and I'm confident I can do the same for you.

I've found that the easiest way to mitigate some of alcohol's negative effects on one's blood sugar and liver is by using whole food ingredients as mixers instead of processed commercial products. Not only does this remove hangover-causing corn syrup and preservatives from the equation, but it adds many foods that have healthful properties that lessen the damage that alcohol can do to your system. For instance, did you know that ginger is a powerful anti-inflammatory and nausea reducer, lemon detoxifies the liver, and fresh green juice is full of vitamins and minerals? This book is full of real foods with amazing healing properties, and these foods don't contain any of the usual artificially flavored ingredients most people are accustomed to adding. I make it a point to not add any refined sugars or gluten ingredients, and I promise that the recipes are all the tastier for it!

Using these whole foods as mixers is not only healthful and harm-reducing, it's ridiculously easy. A box grater or microplane is the only grating tool you'll need, and while a citrus squeezer or reamer is helpful, a fork will do in a pinch. These recipes are accessible and remarkably similar in flavor to their toxic commercial counterparts. In the same vein that I've taught America how to eat more healthfully without sacrificing taste or presentation, in this book I want to show you how to have a relationship with cocktails in which you'll look good, feel great, and regret nothing. If eating well can and should be joyful, drinking should be no different!

Let's Prep

In a perfect world, at the end of the night, you'll feel as if you consumed just the right amount of alcohol. You'll be feeling nice and relaxed but nowhere near sloppy, and you'll awake bright-eyed and bushy-tailed in the morn. In case you think that perfect world doesn't exist or you don't know how to navigate it yourself, let's talk about what to do before, during, and after drinking so that you awake regret-free. Drinking water continuously is a given, of course.

When you know you'll be having an evening out, be conscious of what you eat at dinner, and choose foods that are higher in protein and that don't have a lot of refined carbs. The more refined foods you eat, the more "soakable" food there is in your system and the more alcohol it will take for you to feel a buzz. Choose carbs, like root vegetables or whole grains, that are high in fiber. If your goal is to feel buzzed on a budget of just one or two drinks, aim for a lower-carbohydrate dinner. Conversely, if you know it will be a long night and you want to try every cocktail in this book with a group of friends, eat a filling dinner higher in fibrous carbs and keep snacks on hand. Either way, avoid excess fats late in the day, as alcohol will be metabolized first and those will get stored.

The best-laid plans often go awry! If you've had more alcohol than you meant to, there is still hope for you. Let's review healthy foods and supplements to consume before bed so that you'll love life in the morning.

1. **Activated charcoal:** This is the most common supplement used to pull toxins out of your system. Please DON'T take it before you drink, as hangover-preventing products containing it recommend on the label! You'll never get buzzed, just frustrated. Take one or two activated-charcoal pills either while out and feeling tipsy or when you get home. Taking it earlier will tax your system because you still have to process all that booze and you won't even have reaped its happy benefits.

2. **Zeolite:** My choice over activated charcoal is this milder mineral supplement. I find it easier on the stomach, and you can safely take a couple of pills more if needed. I've gone from way too tipsy to perfectly sober after taking a few, drinking a couple of glasses of water, and waiting an hour. Take one or two at the same time as you would activated charcoal, either while still out or once at home, and if an hour later you still feel less than awesome, take an additional one or two. If a situation is way out of control, a few at once is typically fine (and the most effective option). Be sure to avoid activated charcoal or zeolite within a couple of hours of eating because they prevent nutrient absorption.

3. **Coconut water:** I'm going to be a snob here and say the fresh stuff is infinitely better. Not only does it taste like a delicious coconut rather than dirty feet, but when it hasn't been heated, it also naturally retains more vitamins, including the ever-so-important potassium it's full of. Drink eight to sixteen ounces before bed to help prevent a hangover. While it hasn't been scientifically proven to prevent hangovers, it's incredibly hydrating and many people (myself included) will vouch for its effectiveness.

4. *Ginger:* If you've been boozing from the ginger chapter, that's great! If not, make yourself some ginger tea, grate it fresh into soup, or take a couple of capsules to prevent nausea and reduce inflammation.

5. *Eat a snack!* Yes, the food you eat when drunk is going to waste in terms of calorie consumption, but eating something healthy after drinking too much can save you the next day—at least a little bit. The concept that food can "soak up" alcohol only works if the food came first, but having some lean protein will help stabilize your blood sugar, which in turn will help prevent nausea. Try not to eat anything too heavy, as that can disrupt sleep. Water-filled foods such as soup, any produce, and lean proteins are the wisest choices and will do you way more favors than junk food like pizza or nachos.

What if you overdid it to the extent that you aren't up for any bedtime reading and you're trying to keep your eyes focused on this swirling page the painful morning after? Even now there is hope for you to feel free of regrets! Nothing says "hangover cure" like brunch, so what are your best choices? Again, I'm going to say annoyingly that this just depends on your unique body! The following foods have properties that will assist a hangover recovery, but don't go eating anything that sounds nauseating. Only you know what works for you, so pick foods based on what you think sounds easiest on your poor acidified stomach. Note that this is a small selection of my favorite hangover foods; there are many others that can also help.

1. *Eggs:* Without getting too technical, eggs' claim to fame is their cysteine content, which breaks down the toxins alcohol leave behind. They literally help you detox! Don't be a crazy person who only eats egg whites, though; to properly absorb the protein in egg whites, you need the yolks too.

2. *Coconut flour:* If you want to go the sweet route (which I only recommend you do without any actual sugar involved because sugar will provide a spike and, later, a sudden drop in your already low blood sugar), baked goods or pancakes made from coconut flour are an excellent option. It's high in protein and fiber and has a nutty, light flavor.

3. *Tomato juice:* No, I don't mean a Bloody Mary! Tomatoes help with liver function and a glass full of them is an easy way to get a concentrated amount, though, of course, fresh tomatoes are excellent. Just don't add vodka!

4. *Fruit:* While fruit does contain sugar, the fiber will help slow sugar absorption down. Bananas have potassium and B6, guava is crazy high in vitamin C, watermelon is very hydrating, and blueberries are high in antioxidants. That's just the tip of the fruit iceberg. If your stomach isn't up for much, try nibbling on some fruit.

I'm neither a therapist nor a doctor, but I've had some amazing success at helping other people feel better. I hope *The Thinking Girl's Guide to Drinking* will transform your mind-set about alcohol being part of a healthy lifestyle! My goal in writing this book is for you to be motivated to take control of your drinking and to make lots of fabulous, health-inducing drinks yourself, rather than always relying on the outside world and its less healthful commercial ingredients. And if you need a break from the bottle or you don't consume alcohol, I hope you will feel excited by the many mocktail options you'll have to try. Most of all, I hope this book helps you to enjoy yourself when the mood strikes, armed with an arsenal of awesome cocktail options that will leave you feeling happy, healthy, and satisfied.

Let's Drink

That's why we're here, right? Whether you opened this book because you love cocktails but not hangovers or because you don't drink booze but still want to serve beautiful, interesting beverages to your friends and family, I've got you covered. Although the healthful properties of the whole foods I use as mixers are generally agreed upon and established via scientific research, the wellness community has many conflicting opinions about alcohol. Let's review a few of the big concerns the health world has.

1. *Toxic by-products from fermentation:* Some health professionals claim that clear alcohols have less toxins than colored ones and put white wine on a higher pedestal than red wine—and beer. My thoughts: Base your spirit choice on how each makes your unique body feel. Every alcohol has toxins, no question! Even with the antioxidant properties, cardiovascular health value, and other scientifically proven pluses of various wines and spirits, the toxins still exist. But we all react differently to different ones. Personally, I can drink red wine all night, but a single glass of white and I'm asleep in under thirty minutes. So I drink red and pass on the white. Easy as that. Choose what your body most approves of.

2. *It's un-yogic:* In the yoga world, alcohol is simply not part of the lifestyle. Veganism is the preferred diet, and all substances, including caffeine, are to be eschewed unless taken in a medicinal context. Fun fact: I'm a certified Kundalini yoga instructor. Kundalini is a very spiritually involved form of yoga, utilizing postures to prepare the body for deep meditation. Where does my drinking fit into that? I think it's yogic to be human and enjoy life in a responsible way. I also think it's yogic of me to help others find healthier alternatives, in this case alcohol, which is what this book is all about. You can be a modern yogi who has alcohol, as your personal practice is just that: yours. Just as there is no need to smite or stone your neighbor if you're a Christian, you can be yogic without following every ancient guideline.

3. *Alcohol is bad for weight maintenance and is dehydrating:* Yep, totally. As soon as you start drinking, your body's ability to burn fat lessens significantly. So don't do it daily! It's dehydrating, which means it's good to have water in between drinks, or make your drinks with hydrating liquids, such as cucumber juice or coconut water, both of which are included in this book. If you're on a weight-loss mission, stick to mocktails for a while. If you're cool with where you're at, drink responsibly and mentally liken each boozy beverage to a sliver of cake or pie.

It's also important that you choose spirits made from botanicals rather than chemicals as often as possible. If you're concerned that the specific alcohols in these recipes may be hard to find because they're made out of more "real" ingredients than the liquors you're used to, rest assured, they're all widely commercially available. For instance, though Cynar isn't terribly well known to the home mixologist, it's easy to find and is made from artichoke leaves and herbs. It also only takes a little drop to get big flavor, so a $25 bottle will last a long time!

The main takeaway here is that drinking alcohol more healthfully is possible, especially when done mindfully. When you do imbibe, exercise caution and take it slow—the power of hard liquor trumps any healthful ingredients when overconsumed.

Bar Basics

Tips and Techniques

For this book's cocktail recipes I've partnered with Brittini Rae, a killer bartender who didn't become known as the best female bartender in America just because she's good at her job; she literally won the title when she was crowned winner of the national Speed Rack female bartending competition, and has since trained other women throughout the country on how to best compete. Brittini has created cocktail menus for a host of bars and she knows all of the bar-industry standards. Together, we bring you an at-home mixology experience combining the best of both worlds! These are Brittini's tips and techniques to help you be the most efficient at-home bartender you can be, and you'll find other helpful bartending tips throughout this book.

- Always store your booze in a cool, dry place away from heat and direct sunlight. Read the back labels on bottles with a lower alcohol by volume (ABV), such as vermouth and sherry, to see if it mentions the need for refrigeration after the bottle's been opened.

꙰ Although it's not required, when Brittini sets up her ingredients to make a cocktail, she likes to chill the glassware in the refrigerator or freezer, especially martini and champagne saucers. It's a nice gesture of hospitality and will keep drinks colder longer.

꙰ Be careful to measure your alcohol accurately with a jigger or a measuring spoon! Some ingredients are very strong and can affect the balance of the drink more than you might think.

꙰ Avoid substituting ingredients if at all possible, as using a substitute ingredient when making your cocktail will result in a different and possibly unwanted flavor.

꙰ Each recipe in this book yields one drink, but can easily be doubled, quadrupled, et cetera, if you're making more than one drink or a big batch for a party.

꙰ Both shaking and stirring a cocktail will chill and dilute your drink, so how do you know when to do which? An easy, foolproof rule is to shake when you need to mix citrus and other non-alcohol-based ingredients with your base spirit(s), and to stir when all you are working with is pure alcohol. Shaking with ice creates air bubbles and allows the citrus and alcohol to mix together more easily. You don't need this added effect when you are only mixing alcohols.

꙰ *Double straining* is a technique using both the Hawthorne strainer and a fine-mesh strainer to help filter out all the bits and particles of muddled herbs and unwanted ice chips. We don't use this technique much in this book because of my love for food pieces in drinks, but you may if you prefer silkier beverages.

꙰ To increase the aroma of certain herbs, such as mint and basil, we like to "smack" them: Place the leaves in the palm of one hand and gently hit them with your other hand. This will release essential oils without bruising the leaves.

⌒ To make and use a standard twist, use a sharp paring knife or a Y-shaped peeler to peel a 1–inch-wide and about 3–inch-long zest from your citrus, avoiding the pith (it adds unwanted bitterness to your drink). Express the oils from the citrus zest over your cocktail by pinching the ends, then rim the drink with your peel and drop it in!

⌒ *Muddling* is when you utilize a muddler or the end of a spoon to forcefully press down on herbs, vegetables, or fruits to extract flavors or oils that cannot be achieved by simply shaking the cocktail.

⌒ *Flaming* is when you pinch or squeeze the zest of a citrus fruit over a lit flame in order to light the oils; this caramelizes the oils and adds a great aromatic element to your cocktail. Please exercise caution when flaming citrus peels.

Glassware

The following is a list of the glassware that we recommend using.

All-purpose wineglass: Most commonly used for wine, but it can also be a great substitute for highballs, fruity drinks, punches, and frozen drinks.

Champagne saucer: A stemmed glass for cocktails, most commonly used for drinks that have been chilled and are served "up" without ice.

Collins glass: Slightly taller and usually narrower than a highball glass.

Highball glass: A tall, narrow glass that typically houses a simple blend of spirits and carbonated mixers.

Mason jar: A staple in this book, a mason jar creates a unique look for cocktails and is also an inexpensive and great mixing vessel!

Old-fashioned or rocks glass: A short, versatile glass that can be used for serving spirits with or without ice or for cocktails over ice. It can also supplement as a shot glass.

Other useful but not necessary glassware:

Champagne flute: An elegant stemware with a thin profile that holds the champagne's effervescence.

Sherry or cordial flute: Miniature stemware that is curved so as to hold and enhance the aromatics of delicate fortified wines and cordials.

Shot glass: A small glass, typically about 1½ ounces, from which a spirit or a cocktail is meant to be consumed in one gulp.

Equipment

The following is a list of the equipment that we used to make the drinks in this book.

Accoutrements: This includes sip sticks, straws, cocktail napkins, coasters, cocktail picks, and paper umbrellas, all of which add to a fun presentation.

Bar spoon: A long-handled, shallow spoon with a twisted handle used for stirring drinks or measuring small amounts of liquid.

Blender: Used to make frozen drinks, purée fruit, or even crush ice. A high-powered blender such as a Vitamix or Blendtec is optimal but not required.

Bottle opener and corkscrew: Necessary tools in any kitchen to help with glass beer bottles and wine bottles sealed with a wooden cork.

Citrus juicer: Fresh-squeezed citrus is essential in creating delicious cocktails at home! You don't need an electric juicer, as a hand-operated one will work just fine; you can find a metal or ceramic press at almost any grocery store. Ones that will accommodate multiple sizes of citrus work best.

Cutting board: Commonly made of either wood or plastic, it is used for cutting citrus as well as fruits and vegetables for garnishes.

Hawthorne strainer: The best all-purpose strainer, the Hawthorne features a semicircular spriglike coil that fits perfectly into your mixing vessels to separate ice, muddled fruits, and herbs from your finished cocktail.

Ice scoop: Highly recommended to help transport ice from your ice storage device to your cocktail glass and mixing vessel.

Jigger: A two-sided, stainless-steel measuring device for precise mixing. You will typically need more than one to have all the right measurements, but the Leopold jigger from Cocktail Kingdom has all the measurements in one!

Julep strainer: A perforated, spoon-shaped strainer to use in conjunction with smaller tins and mixing glasses.

Mesh strainer: A fine-mesh strainer is used in addition to other strainers to remove smaller bits and pieces of herbs and ice.

Microplane: A fine-tooth metal grater that is useful for zesting fruit or grating spices like nutmeg and cinnamon.

Mixing glass: A heavy-bottomed glass that is used for mixing cocktail ingredients with ice without creating air bubbles or excessive dilution. A classic favorite is called a Yarai mixing glass, but a widemouthed mason jar will work just fine as well.

Muddler: Similar in shape to a pestle, a muddler is a sturdy tool used to press and crush herbs and fresh fruits.

Paring knife: A small, sharp knife used to prepare fruit and vegetables for garnishes.

Shaker: Used to mix cocktail ingredients with ice; the more commonly known Boston Shaker is a two-piece set that consists of a 16-ounce mixing glass and a slightly larger tin. However, the shaker nicknamed Tin on Tin has now gained a larger following and is our recommendation. This set consists of two metal tins, holding roughly 18 ounces and 28 ounces.

Y peeler: A wide peeler that can be used for making twists and zests from citrus-fruit peels.

LIVER-LOVING

Lemons
AND
Limes

From a twist to a squeeze to a whole lot of satiating sour, lemons and limes are nutritional powerhouses of liver detoxification that also happen to pair well with nearly any alcohol. To reap all the benefits you can from these guys, be sure to squeeze fresh ones and do not use that weird processed bottled stuff. The ways to use lemons and limes are manifold, so let's take advantage of them all!

Citrus is the most commonly used mixer and will be found in recipes throughout this book, but the recipes in this particular section highlight the flavors of lemons and limes as well as their health benefits. For instance, did you know that lemon and lime peels contain pectin, which helps to slow down the absorption of sugar into the body? That means that by grating them finely enough in your beverage, you're actually going to improve your body's ability to deal with the blood-sugar implications of the drink you're consuming.

Because pesticides are sprayed topically, please choose organic lemons and limes when you plan to zest or utilize the peel. Lemon extract is also included here, and you may be wondering how an extract could possibly be beneficial. Extracts are made from concentrated oils, making lemon extract a powerful tool for slowing microbial growth, which is excellent for helping to prevent the candida that drinking can lead to as well as for reducing stress levels in the brain. Sipping on sours has never been so rewarding!

Lime Sublime

Limeade gets an herbaceous make-over with muddled rosemary, a lemongrass stirring stick, and a base of Leopold Bros. Three Pins Alpine Herbal Liqueur, which is a solid 70 proof. The liqueur, though you may not have heard of it, is available at liquor stores and contains ingredients such as echinacea, ginkgo biloba, and orange zest. That's the same echinacea that's used in cold remedies and the same ginkgo biloba that's common in focus-enhancement supplements. Rosemary is known to stimulate the immune system, improve digestion, and help with concentration. Can a cocktail keep you from catching a cold? I'm not sure, but I'm more than happy to help you test out that theory.

1 6-inch sprig rosemary, plus 1 sprig for garnish

2 ounces Leopold Bros. Three Pins Alpine Herbal Liqueur

½ ounce fresh lime juice

2 to 3 dashes celery bitters

Sparkling mineral water, to top

1 lemongrass stirring stick, for garnish

Remove the leaves from the rosemary sprig and place them in a shaker. Discard the stem.

Add the remaining ingredients (except the sparkling water and garnish) to the shaker.

Add ice and shake well.

Strain and pour into a highball glass filled with fresh ice.

Top with sparkling water.

To garnish, place the rosemary sprig and the lemongrass stick in the glass.

Vegas Showgirl

Nothing says *celebration* like champagne; sadly for many people, nothing says *headache* like champagne, either. That's because the carbon dioxide in carbonated drinks speeds up the body's alcohol absorption, leading to higher blood and brain alcohol levels quicker. One way to mitigate this is by drinking flat champagne, but Lord knows none of us want to do that! Instead, by introducing some lemon essence into the mix, we will lend a helping hand to counter a little of that carbonation effect. This drink is simple yet delivers a much-more complex and unique flavor than your usual glass of bubbly. The salt-rim garnish also adds an unusual, and pretty, flair.

1 tablespoon kosher salt, for garnish

1 tablespoon finely ground lemon zest, for garnish

Peel of 1 entire lemon

5 ounces champagne

Prepare the garnish by mixing the kosher salt and lemon zest on a plate.

Muddle the lemon peel in a cocktail shaker until it's broken down into small pieces and smells very aromatic. If needed, add enough water or neutral spirit such as vodka to help with the muddling process.

Add the champagne to the shaker with the muddled peels.

Wet the rim of a champagne flute and dip it into the salt and zest mixture.

Strain into the salt-rimmed flute.

THINKING Girl's NOTE

Brittini prefers rimming only half the glass. That way you can decide as you drink if you want to taste the garnish or not. I love this idea because it involves less commitment and I tend to feel oversalted or oversugared easily. It also makes for a more interesting presentation.

Lemon Halfsies
Martini

Everyone wants to look cool, but we don't all possess the cojones to chug glasses of gin or vodka all night. Thus, a standard martini evening is a viable option only to the select few who can stomach it. For the rest of the population, there's the 50/50 one: equal parts gin or vodka and vermouth. We've made this delicious drink more interesting with a lemon extract rinse. While the lemon isn't overpowering, it's prevalent, and since the extract is so concentrated, you'll still receive its benefits in the beverage. Squeezing a lemon peel over the top of the drink adds a fresh, bright aroma as well as additional volatile oil compounds.

2 dashes lemon extract

1½ ounces gin

1½ ounces French dry vermouth

1 large slice of lemon peel

Pour the lemon extract into a martini glass and swirl it around. Discard the remaining liquid.

Put the gin and vermouth in a mixing glass with ice and stir gently.

Strain into the martini glass.

Squeeze the lemon peel around the rim of the glass.

THINKING Girl's NOTE

The halfsies martini is more common in craft cocktail bars because of its lower alcohol content; if you ask for one at a "regular" bar, they might not be familiar with the concept.

Sweet on Sour in the Tropics

If you read the label on a bottle of sour mix, you'd likely be horrified. Not only does it typically contain high-fructose corn syrup and artificial colors, it's also got whacked-out preservatives, gums, and other unpronounceables. I love my easy homemade version of a whiskey sour made with bourbon, fresh lemon juice, and lemon stevia, but Brittini had a brilliant idea to transform this recipe from a simple sour into something reminiscent of a Cameron's Kick, which utilizes orgeat syrup. Since I don't expect people to spend half a day making a syrup, I came up with a two-minute version that offers a similar flavor profile with less work and, of course, no refined sugar. The result is a cocktail that tastes as classic as it does tropical and refreshing.

2 ounces bourbon

¾ ounce orgeat syrup (page 248)

¾ ounce fresh lemon juice

2 whole unsalted almonds, for garnish

Put all the ingredients (except the garnish) into a shaker with ice and shake well.

Strain into a champagne saucer.

To garnish, drop the almonds into the bottom of the glass.

Cute in Coral

Sure, you could be pretty in pink instead, but I prefer life on the edgy side. The coral color of this drink screams so many awesome things, like *sunshine* and *brunch*. If raspberries are accessible year-round where you live, liven up a dreary winter day with this summer-inspired cocktail. If they aren't and you still want to enjoy it during the off-season, frozen raspberries are an acceptable substitute. They retain the vitamin C, fiber, pantothenic acid, and all the rest of the great things this fruit has to offer. Organic raspberries have a higher antioxidant count, making them the better choice (for that and many other reasons) whether fresh or frozen.

12 raspberries

2 ounces vodka

¾ ounce vanilla syrup (page 248)

¾ ounce lemon juice

1 dash lemon extract

1 lemon wheel, for garnish

Put all the ingredients (except the garnish) into a cocktail shaker and fill with ice.

Shake well and pour directly into a highball glass or mason jar.

Garnish with the lemon wheel.

THINKING Girl's NOTE

For "shake and dump" style drinks (drinks that require a cocktail shaker and use the same ice in the final drink), Brittini recommends filling the glass you'll be serving the cocktail in with ice and then dropping that ice into the shaker. That way you'll know how much ice will fit perfectly in the glass!

Lavender Spa Lemonade

When I came up with the concept for this drink, I was doing it for the sake of the status quo: I felt like the chapter needed a spa-style drink. I kind of hate lavender because it often tastes soapy to me, I'm not big on cucumber, and gin and I are barely acquaintances. Yet somehow these ingredients that I'm not huge on came together in a shockingly delicious way! If you like them to begin with, you'll be even more blown away by this cocktail. Brittini's addition of cucumber to my initial concept brought it all together in a beverage that's a seriously comprehensive experience. Not wanting to detract from lavender's benefits of stomach soothing, nerve calming, and bloat reduction, I kept the quick lavender syrup sugar-free. If you need a spa-day getaway, look no further.

2 ounces American/New Western gin

¾ ounce lavender syrup (page 248)

½ ounce fresh lemon juice

1 tablespoon lemon zest

1 cucumber slice and 1 sprig lavender, for garnish

Shake all the ingredients (except the garnish) with ice in a cocktail shaker.

Strain into a rocks glass filled with fresh ice.

To garnish, place the cucumber slice and the lavender sprig in the glass.

If Wishes Were Green (MOCKTAIL)

Sweet mocktails are a yummy thing, but so are savory ones! Green juice can be an intense experience; consider this its superlight cousin. Limes often get overshadowed by lemons, but they've been used for ages in medicinal ways ranging from aiding digestion to assisting peptic ulcers. The lime zest and juice provide a double dose of taste and health promotion. Muddling sage into the drink releases its volatile oils, which are antifungal, antimicrobial, disinfecting, and anti-inflammatory. In case you were concerned, fear not: It's herbal in flavor, but the sage isn't powerful enough to make the mocktail taste like Thanksgiving stuffing!

12 fresh sage leaves

1 ounce fresh lime juice

2 teaspoons lime zest

Sparkling mineral water, to top

Muddle the sage with the lime juice, then add to a Collins glass filled with ice.

Sprinkle the lime zest in.

Top with sparkling water.

Kimmy Gimlet (MOCKTAIL)

If you've got a full house, chances are that at least a few people in it want something besides a cocktail, and they might not necessarily want a bubbly beverage that's going to take an hour to glug down. By offering up this little bright green gimlet that doesn't actually contain any vegetable juice, you'll set your skills apart from all the other hostesses out there with only spritzers and soda in their repertoire. In addition to the detoxifying lime juice, fresh basil protects against free radicals and can help slow down the aging process and maple syrup sweetens up the drink with a host of added minerals.

12 basil leaves, plus 1 for garnish

2 ounces fresh lime juice

½ ounce maple syrup

Muddle the basil leaves with an ice cube in a cocktail shaker until well broken down.

Add the lime juice and maple syrup to the shaker, then fill it halfway with ice.

Shake to chill and then pour it neat into a shot glass.

To garnish, place the basil leaf on top.

Bitters have made their way into the cocktail mainstream in recent years, which is surprising only because the original bitters brands such as Angostura were initially created as medicines, not for enjoyment.

Once relegated to the background of mixology, used only as an occasional dash in a classic cocktail that required it, or mixed with a simple soda as a digestif, the craft cocktail movement has helped launch bitters into the foreground. Now there are entire lines of organic bitters with flavors ranging from herbal to citrus to chili-chocolate. The bitters umbrella is a larger one than many people realize, including Campari, Aperol, and amari.

In this chapter we also use digestion-stimulating ingredients such as aquavit, food-grade bitter orange essential oil, and Cynar. As drinking typically falls in the evening, adding alcohol to a stomach full of food can be a less than pleasant experience. Drinks with digestive properties help mitigate that discomfort, and digestive mocktails make perfect post-dinner sippers too. Additionally, many of the alcohols in this chapter are full of fascinating herbs and barks that have myriad health benefits!

The Breakup Diet

I'm not at all suggesting that if you recently had a breakup you should head to the liquor cabinet! Rather, the title came to me because breakups can lead one to feel both sour and bitter, and I wanted to share a way in which sour and bitter are actually a good thing. This cocktail blends the tartness of fresh grapefruit juice, which has lots of vitamins A and C and potassium, with grapefruit bitters, our beloved Carpano Antica herb-laden vermouth, and mezcal. The end result is smoky from mezcal, sweet via Carpano, sour with grapefruit juice, and just a touch bitter. The difference between squeezing a grapefruit and opening a jar is one mere minute of effort that I promise you won't regret once you taste the difference!

2 ounces mezcal Espadín

1 ounce grapefruit juice

¾ ounce Carpano Antica

1 dash grapefruit bitters

1 rosemary wreath, for garnish

Shake all the ingredients (except the garnish) with ice in a shaker.

Strain and serve in a champagne saucer.

Garnish with the rosemary wreath.

Notes on Flying

One of my favorite cocktails, the Paper Plane, is made with two types of bitters. It's composed of bourbon, lemon juice, Aperol, and amaro. I add a touch of extra healthiness to my version with a couple of drops of organic food-grade bitter orange essential oil, which adds a stronger orange flavor. Bitter orange oil is an antidepressant, contains d-limonene (which has been studied extensively as a cancer preventative) and helps eliminate toxins. Essentially, it helps you detox as you retox, and that leaves you one bit less toxic in the end! I also switch out the sweet Aperol for the more bitter Campari, the full recipe for which is a secret. It is widely known that the liqueur contains ginseng, which is excellent for brain function, and that it no longer contains cochineal (aka bug juice) for color, making it acceptable now for vegans.

¾ ounce bourbon

¾ ounce Campari

¾ ounce Amaro Nonino

¾ ounce fresh lemon juice

2 drops bitter orange oil

Shake all the ingredients with ice in a shaker.

Strain and serve in a champagne saucer.

Peachy Keen

While there's nothing at all wrong with an old-fashioned, it's *always* a joy to find new fashions! Here, the cocktail gets a little makeover by substituting white sugar for the more healthful coconut sugar. Because the coconut sugar adds a caramel note of flavor, we decided to play on that with some extra bitters. Peach was the winning choice, but feel free to use any other fruit you enjoy that melds well with coconut sugar and bourbon. This drink is small but potent and is therefore best sipped slowly; it tastes like a strong, digestion-enhancing dessert in a glass. It's becoming more popular to use two types of bitters in one drink, though bartenders would still be unlikely to use three.

5 dashes peach bitters

2 dashes Angostura bitters

½ teaspoon coconut sugar dissolved in ½ teaspoon water

2 ounces bourbon

1½-inch-wide lemon peel slice, for garnish

In a rocks glass, add the bitters to the dissolved coconut sugar and muddle briefly to ensure that no crystals remain.

Add the bourbon and stir. Serve neat or with a jumbo cube.

Squeeze the lemon peel over the drink to release volatile oils and drop it in the glass.

Totally Herbaceous

Cilantro is likely one of the most polarizing herbs around: Some people actually have a gene that makes it taste soapy, leaving them unable to enjoy its unique flavor and health properties. Fun fact: I am totally one of those people, and I can't stand it! That said, I understand how much others love cilantro, and I also understand that it's crazy good for you. It helps you detox excess metals and relieve anxiety, and it is chock-full of antioxidants. I've livened up a standard bitters and soda digestif with its addition and swapped out Angostura for Swedish herb bitters, which generally contain eleven herbs that stimulate the liver and circulation, and restore acid balance in the stomach—and that's just a few of its benefits! This herbaceous version of bitters and soda is decidedly more interesting than the usual, and can also do more for you.

5 sprigs cilantro, stems discarded

3 dashes Swedish herb bitters

Sparkling water, to fill

Lime peel, for garnish

Muddle the cilantro in a highball glass with the bitters.

Fill the glass with ice and add the sparkling water to top.

Express the lime peel across the rim of the glass and place it across the top.

Halfsies Herbtini

In the lemon and lime chapter I espoused my newfound love for a 50/50 martini, aka a martini composed of equal parts vodka or gin and vermouth (page 34). Confession: I got a little hooked on this way of making martinis, and in later chapters Brittini basically had to pry the vermouth out of my hands to get me back to using normal proportions. Here, however, she let me ride the halfsies train into Bitter Town, and I think you'll love the results as much as I do. Celery bitters was popular in the pre-Prohibition era and is just now making its way back to popularity. The flavor is complex, at once both herbal and savory; if you use too much things can go terribly awry, but with the proper amount it is a little gulp of heaven. Though different in taste from the standards, celery bitters contains all the usual bitters benefits, such as soothing bloating, relieving heartburn, and balancing blood sugar.

1½ ounces vodka

1½ ounces Italian vermouth

4 dashes celery bitters

3 Castelvetrano olives, for garnish

Stir all the ingredients (except the garnish) in a mixing glass with ice.

Strain into a martini glass and garnish with the olives.

Aqua Camp

Campari, the citrus and herbal bitters liqueur, makes a double appearance in this chapter because it is so well suited to the theme—once just didn't seem enough. Here, it is paired with aquavit, which changes things up drastically, as well as that monk-loving sweet liqueur Benedictine. Orange peel should be expressed over the top of the glass, which means you will squeeze it to push out its aromatic oils. The result of doing this is that when you drink your cocktail, you don't just get the taste of the orange, but the aroma sticks with you too! While drinking the beverage, you'll get a lively mood lift of orange oil.

1½ ounces aquavit

¾ ounce Campari

½ ounce Benedictine

1 orange peel, for garnish

Stir all the ingredients (except the garnish) with ice in a mixing glass.

Pour into a rocks glass filled with fresh ice.

Express the orange peel over the rim of the glass and place it across the top.

THINKING Girl's NOTE

Orange oil is used to counteract depression, and it can turn your frown upside down just by smelling it.

Soda Fountain Delight (MOCKTAIL)

A chocolate cream soda that helps digestion . . . you may be thinking I've gone off the deep end with this one! Fear not, I've got a reasonable basis for the claim, which is that the chili in chocolate chili bitters stimulates digestion. Luckily, the bitters also tastes deliciously chocolaty (no surprise there!) and the vanilla syrup lends a soda fountain flavor that is nothing short of scrumptious and nostalgic. Of course, the syrup is free of refined sugars, as well as full of vanilla to relieve anxiety and stress. Vanilla also aids with nausea, is considered an aphrodisiac, and is used in the beauty industry as an antiaging tool. We use the syrup repeatedly throughout the book, giving you tons of chances to literally get healthier while sipping on a great time. For a brunch where you want a unique drink but no booze, here's a nostalgic glass of happy.

½ ounce vanilla syrup (page 248)

6 dashes chocolate chili bitters

Sparkling mineral water, to fill

Grated dark chocolate, for garnish

In a highball glass, add the syrup and the bitters with ice.

Fill the glass with sparkling water and stir gently.

Garnish with the grated chocolate over the top.

Kombucha-CHA-CHA

When it's time to dance, you'd be well served to make a partner of kombucha! The sparkling probiotic beverage that provides all sorts of good bacteria for your gut comes in a million mixable flavors. How fortunate is that?!

Often, kombucha is not enjoyed because the taste end notes lean on the acerbic side, and people complain that it tastes like vinegar. I've always suggested that the easiest way to combat that finish is to drink it over ice, but adding alcohol and other fun mixers works even better.

Nowadays the flavor options for kombucha are endless; you can find peach, maca root, aronia berry, blue-green algae, rose, and even cola flavor in mainstream and alternative grocery stores. Because kombucha can be tricky to fall in love with, I'm sticking to the fun and childlike side for this chapter, full of easy and delicious tastes. If you already love kombucha, this chapter will be a go-to for you, and if you've been hesitant to try it (or have tried it and did not fall in probiotic love), these drinks provide a painless introduction to the beverage.

Have a Daiquiri with Zachary (MOCKTAIL)

This is like the easy rider of kombucha drinks. At once sweet and tart, the orgeat syrup cuts through any acerbicness of the kombucha with a touch of sweet and tropical, and the lime adds brightness. Strawberry kombucha is a great beginner flavor and reminds many of strawberry soda. Strawberries contain flavonoids that reduce heart attack risk and quercetin for anti-inflammatory benefit, and are suggested to those with high blood pressure for their potassium content. Potassium helps balance sodium; even if you don't have high blood pressure, when consuming a large quantity of sodium (such as the food at most restaurants) it's a great idea to also have high potassium foods for balance.

5 ounces strawberry kombucha

½ ounce fresh lime juice

½ ounce orgeat syrup (page 248)

½ strawberry, for garnish

Fill a mason jar with ice and add the kombucha, lime juice, and orgeat syrup.

Place the strawberry on top for garnish.

Bionic Tonic (MOCKTAIL)

Nowadays most people know how important probiotics are, but not nearly enough people are informed about how important it is to *feed* your probiotics. What do probiotics eat? Why, foods containing prebiotics, of course! There are many foods, such as sunchokes and tiger nuts, that are high in the compounds probiotics thrive upon. Luckily for you, there are no tubers in this mocktail, so it's one you'll actually want to drink! Blackberries, kiwis, and radishes also contain prebiotics and help keep your precious good bacteria population thriving. You may be wondering about the radish, but I promise you that it offers a bitterness akin to adding bitters to a drink. By consuming probiotics and prebiotics together, you're ensuring that your body receives the value of the kefir.

6 blackberries, plus 1 for garnish

½ kiwi, peeled

1 radish, sliced thinly

5 ounces strawberry coconut water kefir, divided

Muddle the 6 blackberries, kiwi, and radish (reserving one slice for the garnish) with 2 ounces kefir in a shaker. Add ice and shake.

Pour the contents into a highball glass and add fresh ice to fill, then pour in the remaining 3 ounces kefir.

Garnish with the radish slice and the blackberry.

Coconut water kefir is widely available in assorted flavors under the Kevita brand; just be warned that they tend to use stevia as a sweetener and it can take a moment to warm up to that, if you haven't already.

THINKING Girl's NOTE

Aphrodisiac Sipper

Damiana is the darling of the Mexican fertility and aphrodisiac world, but it doesn't have very much North American popularity. A woody, mild liqueur, it was supposedly banned at one point in history for being too strong a sex tonic. Clearly, that is no longer considered a problem! While it is produced by several small-batch distilleries, note that the most common and accessible one unfortunately contains artificial colors. It's widely available and is far sweeter than its more legit, harder-to-find, natural counterparts. Peaches are a Japanese symbol of fertility, which makes sense because of their beta-carotene content. Beta-carotene converts in the body to vitamin A, which helps produce the hormones needed for ovulation. That felt like the natural pairing choice for the kombucha flavor for the drink, and I chose mezcal to tie it back into the Mexican theme.

1 ounce Damiana

1 ounce mezcal

Peach kombucha, to fill

Fill a Collins glass with ice and add the Damiana and mezcal.

Stir briefly, then fill with the peach kombucha.

THINKING Girl's NOTE

If you can't find peach kombucha, the more commonly available mango (also full of beta-carotene) makes an equally sexy option.

Upping the Ante

On the one hand, I like to think that I can make absolutely anything better than the store-bought version. On the other hand, I tried repeatedly for months to make good coffee kombucha, and it was mad disgusting every time. I now leave that to the experts, who manage to coax a lightness and freshness out of the drink that I simply could not. Here, we pair this delightful beverage with Pedro Ximénez, a Spanish wine that is considered to be—but does not taste the same as—sherry. It's more syrupy, more complex, and all around more heavenly. Brittini introduced me to it, and you'll see it pop up a whole bunch more in this book because I fell hard in love with its wily ways. Redeye bitters are optional as they are washed with bacon fat and there is no vegan version. You won't be missing anything without it, but if bacony bitters are your thing, they add a yummy breakfast touch. This cocktail is low in alcohol, moderate in caffeine, and high in blissed-out feelings.

5 ounces coffee kombucha

2 ounces Pedro Ximénez

2 dashes redeye bitters, optional

Pour all the ingredients into an old-fashioned glass and stir briefly; serve up.

Crushing in Concord

Having grown up in rural Massachusetts, I spent years going to summer camp next to the Welch's factory. I've since learned that Concord grape flavor is nostalgic even to those who never saw the purple palace in person. (Okay, fine, that's a lie. The building was a normal color, I just couldn't resist the alliteration opportunity.) When choosing a vodka for this drink, if you're sticking with gluten-free selections I recommend a grape vodka over a potato one, for the obvious reason—I love themes, though the taste won't be dramatically different. Ginger liqueur is included to offset the risk of this tasting too much like a bad college party. As ginger aids digestion, it's a natural match with kombucha in terms of the health value, and the flavors meld well together.

1½ ounces vodka

½ ounce ginger liqueur

Grape kombucha, to fill

Pour the vodka and ginger liqueur into a champagne flute.

Fill with the kombucha.

We recommend using a craft version of grape vodka—no need to settle for Ciroc!

THINKING
Girl's
NOTE

Green Light District (MOCKTAIL)

Basil is one of the simplest tools for changing the entire taste of a drink. Just a handful of leaves muddled into some liquid lends a herbaceous, savory, lightly licorice essence. Basil also adds anti-inflammatory and antibacterial properties! Citrus kombucha is basically just plain kombucha plus lemon juice, so don't expect too much complexity from this simple mocktail. What you will get is a savory treat that is refreshing and alluring, sans excessive sweetness. You can also try this with a different herb if you'd like, such as savory, which offers antiseptic and antifungal properties.

6 basil leaves, plus 1 for garnish

5 ounces citrus kombucha, divided

Add the 6 basil leaves to a Collins glass and muddle with 2 ounces kombucha until broken down.

Fill the glass with ice and the remaining 3 ounces kombucha.

Garnish with the basil leaf.

I'm Toasted

What would a summer barbecue be without that delicious smoky aroma in the air? I am one of those smoke-loving people, so genmaicha tea and genmaicha kombucha are regular beverages in my world. Made of toasted rice added to green tea, it gives you all the flavor and antioxidants of standard green tea with an added toasty bonus. Islay scotch is the perfect cohort for this kombucha, which is the type of scotch known for its strong notes of peat and smoke. The orange zest is added for balance and pectin, then the peel is flamed (a technique that is of course optional, but I encourage you to try it!) to bring a charred citrus bite to the cocktail. Note that since Islay scotches are all made from barley, you'll need to use Nikka Whisky instead for a mostly gluten-free-guaranteed option. The smokiness will still shine through! Nikka is 97% corn and 3% barley, so there is still some risk of gluten contamination even though the industry considers all gluten to be distilled out.

5 ounces genmaicha kombucha (substitute green tea kombucha if unavailable)

1½ ounces Islay scotch

½ ounce Cointreau

2 tablespoons orange zest

1 orange peel, for garnish

Fill a mason jar with ice and add all the ingredients except for the orange peel. Stir briefly.

Flame the orange peel over the drink and place it on top to garnish.

Magic Carousel

It's a float, it's a cocktail, it's . . . full of gluconacetobacter kombuchae! So, what in the world is that? Gluconacetobacter kombuchae is a bacteria produced in the kombucha-making process that creates gluconic acid, an acid that combats yeast, thus leading to improved digestion by way of lower candida levels. Kombucha also contains similar-sounding glucuronic acid, which binds to toxins in the liver and removes them via the kidneys. In human terms, that means kombucha helps you release toxins when you pee, and it can help with yeast infections. In the spirit of desserts and awesomeness, I combined root beer kombucha with vanilla ice cream and whiskey. Feel free to use your favorite ice cream brand, or be a renegade and make your own if you've got some time to kill. If there is any way to get used to the taste of something new, drowning it in ice cream and hard liquor is for sure the smoothest way to go.

1 large scoop vanilla ice cream

2 ounces whiskey

Root beer kombucha, to fill

Scoop the ice cream into a sundae glass.

Pour the whiskey over the ice cream, then fill the glass with the kombucha.

There's no need to sacrifice our good looks just because we want to get tipsy! Collagen protein is available commercially as a superfine powder that blends into any liquid, cold or hot, and has no taste at all. It doesn't alter the texture of the beverage you add it to, either. Since I promised vegan options for all drinks, this chapter is full of collagen-promoting foods for mixers.

Beets, berries, citrus, and white tea are plant-based collagen boosters that are used throughout and will help bring a little extra spring (literally!) to your step. If you aren't vegan, I encourage you to add a tablespoon of collagen powder to each drink for maximum benefit. There's no need to take any extra actions beyond simply shaking or stirring the powder in with other ingredients.

I've found that taking collagen powder regularly has decreased the duration my burns, cuts, and other chef-life calamities take to heal. What used to require a week or more was whittled down to a couple of days, so though I'm not much of a flesh eater, I stick with supplementing collagen. It contains protein and thus helps to balance the sugar in alcohol. No worries if this isn't your bag, though. These drinks contain plenty of collagen-promoting ingredients without the supplement.

Love and Beets

Outside of being devastatingly good-looking, beet juice makes a surprisingly versatile cocktail ingredient. Its earthiness is easily mellowed, which is awesome because the taste of dirt does not a lovely cocktail make. It's important not to drink too much fresh beet juice at once due to its potency as a blood purifier! Because it can be intensely detoxifying, I paired it with a low-alcohol liqueur Crème Yvette, which is essentially a vintage violet dream. It fell out of fashion, as well as production, between the late 1960s and 2009. Back now and gaining in popularity, it is made from violet petals, fresh berries, vanilla, and spices. Mint rounds out the sweetness without overshadowing the delicate floral nature of the Crème Yvette.

1½ ounces fresh beet juice

½ ounce Crème Yvette

6 mint leaves

Shake all the ingredients in a shaker with ice.

Strain into a double shot glass.

Thai Chi

Once upon a time I was a front-of-house manager for a super-fancy Japanese restaurant in San Francisco. This cocktail reminds me of something they would serve. Cranberry juice is best purchased as a fruit juice blend; cocktails with juice have tons of added sugar and straight 100% cranberry juice is essentially unpalatable to most people. There are multiple natural brands that offer a blend sweetened with other juices, leaving the cranberry with enough strength to make its high vitamin C content, which facilitates collagen production, more useful. Nigori, an unfiltered sake, gives the drink its fun opacity. Nigori also contains ferulic acids, which are antioxidants that prevent aging, so it fits in perfectly here! Tangerine oil helps maintain oil and moisture balance in the skin while offsetting the tartness of cranberry.

2 ounces fruit-juice-sweetened cranberry juice, such as Lakewood Organic

1½ ounces nigori sake

1 ounce soju

2 tablespoons orange zest

1 drop food-grade tangerine essential oil

1 orange peel, for garnish

Stir all the ingredients (except the garnish) in a shaker with ice.

Strain into a champagne saucer and garnish with the orange peel.

Feeling Smurfy

While fresh is always best, frozen blueberries are a completely acceptable substitute here and will allow you to make this drink at any time of year. They lose little of their health value through freezing, and the taste when muddled into a drink isn't terribly different. Similar to blackberries, their dark coloring houses high quantities of disease-fighting antioxidants. The anthocyanins in them work alongside vitamin C to strengthen the collagen fibers in your skin, while the copper utilizes that same vitamin C to form elastin, which keeps skin taut. On the one hand, this drink is sweet and delicious and positively Smurfy, and on the other, it just might help you look a little younger!

20 blueberries, plus 4 for garnish

½ ounce fresh lemon juice

¼ ounce vanilla syrup (page 248)

2 ounces American/New Western gin

Sparkling mineral water, to fill

Muddle the 20 blueberries in a shaker with the lemon juice and syrup. Add ice and the gin and shake well.

Fill a highball glass with fresh ice and strain the mixture in, topping with sparkling water until full.

Garnish with the blueberries.

At a bar you'd find a drink like this made with maybe only twelve berries for cost's sake. In our at-home version we add more blueberries, which not only increases the flavor but also the health value.

THINKING
Girl's
NOTE

Beauty Awakening

Equal parts fruity, floral, and herbaceous, this cocktail hits myriad notes of deliciousness. While white tea provides a little lift of caffeine along with protecting skin from UV light and aiding in weight loss, orange juice offers vitamin C for collagen production, and the Leopold Bros. Three Pins Alpine Herbal Liqueur has exciting ingredients like ginkgo biloba and echinacea. Lemon juice provides a touch of tartness while adding its own vitamin C, alkalizing abilities, and copper. If you're unsure about trying a herbal liqueur, this is a good intro to them because the flavors are mellowed by tea and juices.

2 ounces Leopold Bros. Three Pins Alpine Herbal Liqueur

1 ounce fresh orange juice

1 ounce strongly brewed white tea

½ ounce fresh lemon juice

1 lemon peel and 1 rosemary sprig, for garnish

Shake all the ingredients (except the garnish) with ice in a shaker.

Strain into a rocks glass filled with fresh ice and garnish with the lemon peel and rosemary sprig.

You Look Marvelous Martini

Tea in general is a health powerhouse, and each type has its own unique offerings. White tea is light and floral in taste, and strong in the ways in which it will love you and your body. It's popular as a tool for healthy skin, but it is also excellent for relieving diabetes symptoms, improving oral health, and it retains more antimicrobial properties than green or black tea due to more minimal processing. It takes just a minute or two to brew, so there isn't too much advanced planning required. I recommend using just a few ounces of water per tea bag in order to yield at least one-fourth the brewed amount in your martini. Blackberries don't only give a gorgeous color and a collagen-building ability to the drink but have also one of the highest antioxidant levels of all fruits due to their intense black color.

6 blackberries, plus 1 for garnish

1 ounce strongly brewed white tea

½ ounce elderflower liqueur

1½ ounces London Dry gin

Muddle the 6 blackberries with the white tea in a shaker until broken down.

Add the elderflower liqueur and gin with ice and stir.

Strain into a martini glass and garnish with the blackberry in the bottom of the glass.

So Bloody Lovely (MOCKTAIL)

Ginger improves the healing time of wounds and is used in face serums to promote collagen production. Here, it's used fresh in the homemade ginger beer on page 104, which counters the sweetness of beet juice by adding some spice. The lime in the ginger beer provides extra complexity as well as flavanoids to keep skin shiny and reduce body odor. Since beet juice is so potent a blood purifier, two ounces is sufficient. However, as we aren't pairing it with alcohol in this beverage, if you're used to drinking beet juice and are accustomed to its effects, you may wish to try a high proportion of it (or use a larger glass to add more). The color is a gorgeous magenta, making it a great pick-me-up both in looks and benefits.

2 ounces fresh beet juice

5 ounces Lava Sparks Ginger Beer mocktail (page 104)

1 slice ginger, for garnish

Fill a highball glass with ice and add the beet juice and ginger beer.

Stir briefly to combine and garnish with the ginger slice.

Bloody Lovely, Lighter

(MOCKTAIL)

Can't be bothered to make ginger beer? Not a problem! I've combined fresh beet juice with super-simple sparkling mineral water, and the result is sweet spa seduction. You can get a solid portion of your body's RDA of calcium from mineral water, making this drink good from skin to bones. Mineral water also contains a decent amount of magnesium, which offsets the sugar content of beet juice a bit by helping to regulate your blood sugar. Beet juice was used in ancient Rome as an aphrodisiac, something that has since been legitimized by its boron content (boron plays a role in the production of sex hormones) and by betaine, which relaxes the mind. Outside of that, this drink is a way cool magenta color that is just plain delightful to drink.

2 ounces fresh beet juice

5 ounces sparkling mineral water, to fill

1 slice ginger, for garnish

Fill a highball glass with ice and add the beet juice and sparkling water.

Stir briefly to combine and garnish with the ginger slice.

Sour Smash Sweetly

Raspberries are the easiest berry to make cocktails with because their delicate nature leads them to break down into a drink with very little effort. If you shake them with ice, there's no need to muddle! Fresh or frozen, they've got a top ORAC rating, meaning that their antioxidant content is among the highest of all fruits. Though beautifully scarlet in presentation, there is no sweetener in this cocktail outside of the sweetness of Byrrh, so the drink errs on the tangy side. The aperitif Byrrh was banned in the United States from Prohibition until 2012, and it is flavored with cinchona, a bark used to make quinine. Quinine, most commonly known as the main flavor of tonic water, is used medicinally in stronger dosages. In Byrrh, the quinine content is far milder and not of concern.

12 raspberries, plus 1 for garnish

¾ ounce Byrrh

1½ ounces bourbon

2 lemon wedges

Fill a julep cup with ice. Transfer the ice to a plastic zip-lock bag and crush it with a mallet or hammer; pour the ice into the julep cup.

Shake the 12 raspberries, Byrrh, bourbon, and lemon wedges in a shaker with fresh ice.

Strain into the julep cup and garnish with the raspberry.

As a stand-in for Byrrh, you could substitute it with sweet vermouth.

THINKING
(Girl's)
NOTE

Ginger,
and
I Don't Mean
REDHEADS

nflammation isn't sexy, so thank heavens ginger is tasty! A powerful anti-inflammatory, ginger brings a vibrant and refreshing flavor to drinks. Additionally, it's great for reducing nausea and lowering blood sugar, both of which are perfect weapons to have in your arsenal when consuming booze.

You can play down its flavor by pairing it with sweet mixers and spirits, or play it up with spicier and tangier ones. I'm prone to the latter, though, of course, both are included here so that everyone can enjoy this root's offerings.

Juicing fresh ginger is quick and easy, even without a juicer. Simply grate it (no need to bother peeling!) on a microplane or on the small setting of a box grater. When you have a sufficient amount of pulp accumulated, squeeze it in your hands and let the juice fall into a cup or bowl. This version is a little milder than the overpowering fresh juice you'd get at a juice bar, making it more tolerable for those who aren't into searing spice. These recipes are formulated based on a simple homemade version of ginger juice, so if you purchase ginger juice fresh, use about 25% less than what I call for.

Fire and *Spicy*

If there's one thing I'm not, it's a margarita girl. Tequila did me dirty one time too many in college, and I spent years afterward disliking the taste no matter how many fancy "sipping" ones I was introduced to. Now that it's been about a million years since then, because I only *look* like I might not be pushing forty, college is a hallucinogen-laced blur of history, and tequila and I are casual acquaintances. Still, if I'm going to have a "margie," it needs to have some strong additional notes. This recipe is replete with smoky chili heat and liver-loving lime juice. We chose a homemade ginger syrup for the sweetener along with fresh ginger juice for a double dose of improved cognitive function, enhanced fat digestion, and inflammation-based pain relief.

2 ounces tequila

¾ ounce ginger syrup (page 249)

¾ ounce fresh lime juice

¼ teaspoon fresh ginger juice

2 small shakes of chipotle powder, divided

Shake all the ingredients (reserving 1 shake chipotle powder for the garnish) in a shaker with ice.

Strain into a rocks glass filled with fresh ice and garnish with the additional shake of chipotle powder if the spice level is tolerable.

A standard salt rim isn't necessary because ginger and lime are already balancing the tequila. Also, salt would make the spicy elements potentially seem even hotter, and this drink already has plenty of fire.

THINKING *Girl's* NOTE

Blond Hound

This is a riff off a classic greyhound cocktail. Squeezing a single grapefruit produces just the right amount of liquid per drink and results in a much fresher taste—not to mention many more vitamins! The nutritious fruit contains flavanones to help lower stroke risk and is notoriously helpful for weight management. Fun fact: Grapefruit got its name because it grows in clusters, like grapes. Using homemade ginger beer helps keep the glycemic load down since it's made with coconut sugar and not cane. Fresh ginger juice adds a shot of immune-boosting and cancer prevention, and the combo of ginger and grapefruit is incredibly lively on the palate!

4 ounces fresh grapefruit juice

2 ounces vodka

4 ounces Lava Sparks Ginger Beer mocktail (page 104)

1 grapefruit wheel, for garnish

Pour the grapefruit juice and vodka into a mason jar and stir briefly.

Fill with ginger beer and top with the grapefruit wheel for garnish.

Ginger Scene Queen

Say hello again to our good friend Pedro Ximénez, which, it turns out, gets along famously with ginger and pear. Pear juice might seem a little off the beaten path, but rest assured that it's available through a number of different brands; this is one juice that I don't recommend trying to purchase fresh, as I've never seen it anywhere. Pears lend a boost of copper and vitamin K. Copper is important for healthy babies, so if you're thinking about getting pregnant, it's a good nutrient to make sure you have enough of in your diet, and vitamin K is important for ensuring that you don't get osteoporosis. This drink would be a splendid one to make for a holiday party punch! It's moderate in alcohol and ridiculously high in yumminess. Nutmeg creates an aroma similar to that of eggnog, just in the context of a much lighter drink.

1 ounce fresh pear juice

1 ounce Pedro Ximénez

½ ounce ginger liqueur

1 small pinch ground or grated nutmeg, plus extra for garnish

Shake all the ingredients in a shaker with ice, then strain into a shot glass.

Sprinkle the additional nutmeg over the top.

Cozy Fire

Perfect for a chilly winter's night or for re-creating the vibe of one at any other time of year, this drink is named for how much it makes me want to sip it in front of a roaring fireplace. Spiced rum tends to have more sugar and lower alcohol than straight, so choosing a good quality brand here is particularly important for the avoidance of a sugar-induced hangover. The orange notes of spiced rum are played up with orange bitters, further enhancing the autumnal appeal. Ginger syrup provides plenty of the rhizome since rum tastes spicy too. Bitter orange is excellent for digestion, as is ginger, so this drink also does well as a substitute for dessert.

2 ounces spiced rum

¾ ounce ginger syrup (page 249)

2 dashes orange bitters

Stir all the ingredients briefly in a mixing glass with ice to chill, then strain into a rocks glass with a single large ice cube.

Hotter Toddy

Who in their right mind first thought "Hey, I should add a bunch of hot water to this alcohol," because that's a scrumptious thing to do?! I used to find hot toddies to be stodgy, relegated to those who wanted to go out but had caught a cold so they couldn't drink like normal people. Over the years I've come to appreciate warm beverages, but I still like them a little spruced up. Here, instead of water I use fresh ginger tea, and sugar is swapped out for buckwheat honey (use maple syrup if you're vegan) because it's the highest in minerals and antioxidants of any honey. This drink is fabulously comforting for any friend who is feeling down! The cinnamon oil rounds out the ginger flavor while keeping blood sugar stable, boosting the immune system and soothing the throat.

5 ounces strongly brewed hot ginger tea

2 ounces bourbon

¾ ounce fresh lemon juice

¾ ounce honey or maple syrup

1 drop food-grade cinnamon essential oil

1 cinnamon stick, for garnish

Pour all the ingredients (except the garnish) into a coffee mug and stir to combine.

Add the cinnamon stick as a stirrer to garnish.

To make fresh ginger tea, add several round slices of ginger to a cup of near-boiling water and let steep for 10 minutes.

THINKING *Girl's* NOTE

Ginger Flash

Aquavit is an underused digestif that gets its savory flavor from caraway or dill. It can also contain fennel, cumin, cardamom, and orange peel, and it marries well with ginger and lemon. Caraway is excellent for relieving bloating and protecting the body from free radicals, so that's a little added bonus to aquavit. This drink is a nice alternative to a martini and is super-sippable. It's perfect for an after-dinner drink, especially if you ate a heavy meal; besides the digestive properties of aquavit, ginger has many of its own, including reducing gas. Lemon juice is alkalizing, helping to combat the acidic nature of alcohol, and brings bright flavor to the beverage. While this is a traditional "sour" in terms of proportions, the taste is particularly unique due to the flavor of aquavit.

2 ounces aquavit

½ ounce fresh lemon juice

¾ ounce ginger syrup (page 248)

1 lemon wheel, for garnish

Shake the aquavit, lemon juice, and ginger syrup in a shaker with ice.

Strain into a martini glass and garnish with the lemon wheel.

Firefly Fantasy

As loudly as Cozy Fire (page 98) shouts fall or winter, this drink screams spring and summer. The lavender-ginger combo feels fresh on the taste buds and the only alcohol is ginger liqueur, so it's the sort of drink that would make an acceptable afternoon delight. The lavender sprig garnish adds a delicious floral aroma. Lavender has many of the same properties as ginger, such as pain, nausea, and bloating reduction, but where ginger is warm and invigorating, lavender is soothing and calming. It's used to relieve anxiety, enhance a relaxation experience, and ease the emotional symptoms of PMS. The double dose of ginger between fresh ginger beer and the liqueur balances perfectly with the sugarless, yet still quite sweet, lavender syrup.

1 ounce ginger liqueur

¾ ounce fresh lime juice

½ ounce lavender syrup (page 248)

2 ounces Lava Sparks Ginger Beer mocktail (page 104)

2 sprigs lavender and 1 lime wheel, for garnish

Shake the ginger liqueur, lime juice, and lavender syrup in a shaker with ice.

Strain into a rocks glass filled with fresh ice and top with the ginger beer.

Garnish with the lavender sprigs and lime wheel.

Lava Sparks Ginger Beer (MOCKTAIL)

Ginger beer in a can or bottle can't compare to the homemade version, and making it yourself only takes a couple of minutes! It has a spicy taste and an invigorating effect, so it's very pleasant on its own, outside of its usage as a mixer. Coconut sugar is similar in flavor to brown sugar but is lower on the glycemic index than cane sugar, thus making it the wiser choice. Some say the glycemic index isn't relevant for sweeteners; whether you believe that or not, coconut sugar still has decidedly less fructose than other sweeteners, such as cane sugar, honey, or maple syrup, and everyone agrees that fructose consumption should be minimized.

1 ounce fresh ginger juice

¼ ounce fresh lime juice

2 tablespoons coconut sugar

12 ounces sparkling mineral water, to fill

Shake the ginger juice, lime juice, and coconut sugar in a shaker until the sugar is dissolved.

Pour into a pint glass and fill with the sparkling water, stirring briefly to combine.

THINKING (Girl's) NOTE

Coconut sugar can now be obtained in mainstream stores like Trader Joe's. If you want to make this mocktail ahead of time, don't add the sparkling water until you're ready to drink it. You can also multiply the quantity and add water when ready to consume so that you have it on hand for all of the assorted cocktails it's used in.

Café au

STAY-UP-LAIT

e're full of antioxidants and we aren't gonna sleep on the job! Of course you can use decaf instead, without any change in taste or alcoholic function.

I've been astounded at the number of people who drink chemical- and dye-filled energy beverages, such as Monster or Red Bull, and consider coffee to be a much more natural alternative since it contains only one simple source of short-term energy that most of us are already accustomed to. Coffee drinks can go in two very different directions: creamy and thick with dairylike mixers or translucent with mixers like soda. We've composed recipes for each style of coffee drink, with the focus more on a splash of coffee in a unique drink than on plain cups of coffee spiked with whiskey, because you totally don't need us for that sort of thing!

Since coffee is one of the most pesticide-laden crops on the planet, organic is imperative when choosing your java. And if it's not fair trade, it can also involve some practices like child slave labor that you definitely don't want to be a part of, so it's vital to look for a "fair trade" or similar seal.

Coffee Cake Collins

The dairy/nondairy choice here is up to you, and this cocktail won't suffer no matter what you choose as long as it's sufficiently creamy; I'd avoid a very thin nondairy milk such as rice. Coconut or soy creamers will give you a result similar to whole milk or half-and-half, and almond milk or hemp will have a feel like 2% cow milk. Brittini prefers a creamer over milk, as it gives the drink more body. Orgeat syrup provides a richness that pairs perfectly with rum, and I created the syrup with a potent amount of almond extract so that you get lots of flavor with a smaller amount of sweetener.

3 ounces cold coffee

2 ounces rum

¾ ounce milk, nondairy milk, or nondairy creamer

¾ ounce orgeat syrup (page 248)

Shake all the ingredients in a shaker with ice and strain over fresh ice in a Collins glass.

THINKING Girl's NOTE

For the coffee used here, cold brew is an excellent choice. Not only is it already chilled, it has less acid than standard brewing methods, making it easier on your stomach.

Mocha Truffle Shot

Looking to get the party started but haven't decided which hard alcohol you'll be committing to tonight? This little shot won't make you choose! It only has two low-alcohol liqueurs, so there's no need to chill the alcohol—the shot is perfect at room temp. It's a little chocolaty, a little nutty, and very delicious. Good-quality amaretto utilizes real almonds and/or fruit pits in the process of making it, not artificial flavors. Apricot pits are often used, which contain relatively uncommon vitamin B17 and are heralded as a cure for cancer within holistic communities. Good crème de cacao is made from cacao beans and vanilla beans, and the color comes from those elements rather than caramel coloring. Nutty, chocolate coffee that you don't have to commit to a full glass of? Shoot me one of those, please!

1 ounce warm or room-temperature espresso

¾ ounce crème de cacao

¾ ounce amaretto

Pour all the ingredients into a shot glass and stir to combine.

Caipirinha de Café

Caipirinhas are a fun Brazilian cocktail that took the world by storm in recent years and are steadfastly becoming one of the most popular drinks around. I switched out cane sugar in the cocktail for coconut sugar to reduce the fructose load, rounded that out with a dash of homemade vanilla syrup, and added coffee for riboflavin and pantothenic acid. With a 2-ounce addition of caffeine, there shouldn't be enough coffee here to keep you up too late. If that still seems like too much for you in the evening, though, go decaf; the taste won't change much! Coffee with lime might seem strange, but there is a coffeehouse drink called a Guillermo that is espresso poured over lime wedges. Here, we keep the lime wedges whole as well. Since both ingredients are acidic, it works better than you might think!

2 ounces cachaça

2 ounces cold coffee

¾ ounce vanilla syrup (page 248)

1 teaspoon coconut sugar

4 lime wedges

Shake all the ingredients in a shaker with ice and pour directly into a rocks glass.

Anise, Janice, I Love You

Licorice is another one of those flavors that have strong yeas and nays. I always disliked it until about ten years ago when I fell in love with absinthe. Its kooky effects soon had me craving that anise flavor, and I no longer had an aversion to it. While absinthe is a little too serious for me nowadays, I enjoy other liqueurs with similar tastes (and milder effects), such as sambuca. If you're already a fan, this cocktail will serve you well. If you're not, it totally has the power to sway you! Not only does coffee balance the sambuca, I've thrown in some melted dark chocolate to turn this into a sweet treat. For a brunch alternative to standard mimosas and Blood Marys, this is a perfect option.

1 tablespoon dark chocolate

6 ounces hot coffee

¼ teaspoon vanilla extract

2 ounces sambuca

Melt the chocolate in a saucepan over low heat with the coffee and vanilla extract.

Remove the saucepan from the heat and whisk in the sambuca. Serve hot in a coffee mug.

Since you'd likely have coffee at brunch anyway, we're basically just saving you valuable stomach space for food via this twofer! If there's one thing I understand, it's the value of your tummy's real estate.

THINKING Girl's NOTE

Industry Standard

If you've ever known anyone in the restaurant or bar industry, especially on the West Coast, fernet is, like, The Thing. It's a herbal liqueur that is way stronger than the gentle Leopold Bros. Alpine we use throughout the book, and it is known for its syrupy bitterness. If it's available near you, I'd *definitely* choose the version Brittini recommends in the spirits glossary (page 251), as it is not nearly so much of an assault to one's mouth but rather a touch sweeter and milder. Fernet is so medicinal that it managed to defy Prohibition by remaining available in hospitals! Fernet is called a "bartender's handshake" for its industry popularity.

4 ounces cold coffee

2 ounces bourbon

1 ounce fernet

½ ounce vanilla syrup (page 248)

Shake all the ingredients in a shaker with ice and pour directly into a mason jar.

For the coffee, cold brew would, of course, be your hippest choice. Not only does it contain less acid, but it keeps for much longer and can be refrigerated for days.

THINKING
Girl's
NOTE

Queen of Cups

Falernum, a liqueur that's as fun to say as it is to drink, is a rum-based syrup with a similar flavor profile to orgeat. It differs in that it also has notes of lime and clove rather than the mainly almond tone of orgeat, though almond is prevalent in falernum too. Spanish brandy is often not used because it can be hard to discern a good choice; it's also associated more with your grandparents' libation than with craft cocktails! There are delicious options available, as we detail in the spirits glossary (page 251). Spain is a great area for growing grapes, as evidenced by all the wonderful sherries in the world. The chocolate chili bitters add an extra layer of flavor, plus they cut right through the coffee and brandy to provide a great end note on the palate.

6 ounces hot coffee

1½ ounces Spanish brandy

1 ounce falernum

Scant ¼ teaspoon coffee extract

2 dashes chocolate chili bitters

Pour all the ingredients into a coffee mug and stir to combine.

Sexpresso (MOCKTAIL)

Chill out, rev up, and get ready for a feisty day! Maca is an amazing Peruvian root that works to balance hormones and enhance sex drive for both women and men. While not a huge believer in the stuff initially, I found that after taking it regularly for about six months, my cycle regulated itself for basically the first time ever. Better yet, it lined up to the moon! Unless something goes awry, I'm a new moon bleeder, which is as on track as a hippie chick could be in life. Unfortunately, maca has a lot of indigestible fiber and tends to cause bloating—talk about nullifying the sexy factor! I use Longevity Power Maca Bliss to prevent that, because it's a concentrated extract that has the fiber removed. Same malty taste as regular maca, no weird stomach issues. Here, I add espresso for antioxidants and buzz, and fennel seed for further sex appeal—it's been used as an aphrodisiac for women since ancient Egyptian times.

2 ounces cold espresso

½ ounce maple syrup

1 pinch ground fennel seed

1 teaspoon Longevity Power Maca Bliss powder

Shake all the ingredients in a shaker with ice and strain into a shot glass.

Mock-irinha de Café (MOCKTAIL)

In case you loved the idea of the caipirinha de café but didn't want to go on a date with cachaça, we simplified the recipe into a mocktail. Lime zest adds a unique element to coffee, coconut sugar sweetens it slightly, and sparkling mineral water turns it into a nice bubbly glassful of goodness. This is a light option for any time of day, and feels much more festive than a simple cup of java alone. Did you know that coffee is good for the liver, whether or not it contains caffeine? It was originally assumed that the caffeine content was the reason coffee helped to lower liver enzyme levels, but then further research showed that decaf did the same. It's nice to know that whether you want the caffeine or not, coffee can still treat you kindly!

5 ounces room-temperature coffee

1 tablespoon lime zest

1 teaspoon coconut sugar

Sparkling mineral water, to fill

Shake the coffee, lime zest, and coconut sugar in a shaker with ice and strain into a rocks glass filled with fresh ice.

Top with the sparkling water.

I SCREAM FOR

Coconut

Cream

Coconut will help our brains and our metabolisms, and a proper piña colada couldn't exist without it. Coconut butter is sold in a jar that will likely last you for ages, and I'm prone to using a spoonful of it, along with a blender, to create my own coconut-based liquids such as coconut cream and coconut milk. This eliminates the need for canned coconut milk or cream, since I try to avoid using cans at all in my culinary life, and I can decide with each drink I make exactly how thick and rich (or thin and sippable) I want it to be.

Since coconut lends itself particularly well to blending, this chapter offers multiple blended bevvies to enjoy! They're great to make by the pitcher, and all recipes can be easily multiplied to satiate a gaggle of giggling girls.

One of coconut's main attributes is its concentration of medium-chain triglycerides, a form of fat that don't require metabolism by the liver. They head directly to your brain to give you energy and therefore get stored less easily as fat; hence coconut oil's reputation for aiding in fat burning and boosting metabolism. Coconut is also antifungal, antimicrobial, and anti a whole bunch of other bad things that alcohol consumption can lead to, making it a top food for mitigating booze's negative effects.

Frozen Cherry
Macaroon

Okay, there may be no such cookie as a cherry macaroon. I asked Mr. Google and all he came up with were macaroons with maraschino cherries stuck in the middle, which sounds completely gross, but if there were such a thing, this is what that cookie would be like in cocktail form—it's mad yummy, the color is über-girly, and it's filling enough to double as a snack! Cherries lower your risk of gout, support healthy sleep by way of melatonin production, decrease cancer risk, and lower risk of stroke. Oh, and they're freaking delicious! Buying them frozen is a foolproof way to get around the pit issue and keeps them available year-round.

½ cup fresh or frozen cherries

½ cup coconut milk

½ tablespoon coconut butter

½ cup ice

2 ounces white rum

½ ounce amaretto

2 dashes sour cherry bitters

1 tablespoon toasted coconut chips, for garnish

Blend all the ingredients (except the garnish) in a blender on high speed until smooth and creamy.

Serve in a glass or tiki mug and garnish with the coconut chips.

Buying cherries frozen is my go-to for fruit, and there's no need to feel bad about taking a shortcut when you head to the freezer aisle. They work quite well for this cocktail.

THINKING Girl's NOTE

White Chocolada Martini

Were you ever a fan of the scrumptious sugar headaches known as chocolate martinis? If you loved their taste but not their devastating effects, this drink has your name all over it. Coconut butter adds fiber and a dash of protein, helping you sip this sweet cocktail a little more leisurely. Cacao nibs are a crunchy garnish, but watch out if you're not used to them. Real cacao beans, which cacao nibs are crushed versions of, don't exactly taste like chocolate! They're pretty bitter, though most people love them once they acquire the taste. If they're not your thing, garnish yours with mini chocolate chips or grated chocolate. Chocolate martinis have gotten a bad rap due to the sugary, artificial ingredients like Godiva liqueur; here, we lose the Godiva for a top-quality chocolate-coconut drink.

2 ounces vodka

1 ounce crème de cacao

1 tablespoon coconut butter

1 dash chocolate bitters

5 cacao nibs, for garnish

Shake everything except the cacao nibs in a shaker with ice, then strain into a martini glass.

Garnish with the cacao nibs floating on top.

Dancing Pirates

Coconut water is renowned as a hangover cure due to its electrolyte content, so why not use it as a mixer and help prevent one in the first place?! Typically, when people don't love the flavor, it's because they've been drinking the boxed type. Fresh coconut water is incomparable! It's sweet and delectable, not at all like the pasteurized version that is vaguely reminiscent of feet. The price is worth the effect and the flavor, as a 16-ounce bottle's cost of $5 or so will yield multiple drinks. Combined with detoxifying lemon juice and digestion-enhancing aquavit, this drink is as refreshing as it is healthful. Ginger syrup and elderflower liqueur sweeten things up to get you in a dancing mood that should last for hours.

4 ounces coconut water

2 ounces aquavit

¾ ounce fresh lemon juice

¾ ounce ginger syrup (page 249)

½ ounce elderflower liqueur

1 lemon wheel, for garnish

Shake everything except the lemon wheel in a shaker with ice, then strain into a highball glass filled with fresh ice.

Garnish with the lemon wheel.

If You Like
Piña Coladas

Whether or not you care to get caught in the rain, this cocktail will remind you of the tropics! Rather than using pineapple juice, I opted for whole pieces of the fruit, plus creamy banana, to turn this into a frozen treat that has a ton of whole food value. Even with the banana and the falernum, it's less sweet than what you're likely used to in a piña colada, but I promise you won't miss the excess sugar! The fiber from the pineapple chunks and the banana help to slow down the absorption of sugar into your bloodstream, as well as the absorption of alcohol, so the buzz from this one might take a minute longer to kick in than a drink without blended fruit.

1 cup frozen pineapple pieces

½ cup ice

2 ounces white rum

½ ounce falernum

1½ tablespoons coconut butter

½ frozen banana

Blend all the ingredients in a blender until smooth and creamy and serve in a daiquiri glass.

Kava Milk

Whether to mix the mildly intoxicating herb kava with alcohol or not is a topic of hot debate; apparently it's done regularly in the indigenous cultures that consume the herb, but it is frowned upon in other cultures because the point of it is supposed to be that it's an alcohol alternative. In the other drinks we use it in, there is no booze contained at all (pages 197 and 214), but I did want to include alcohol in at least one drink for those who enjoy the effects of the two together. I certainly don't recommend doing it regularly, as it could be hard on your liver if you have liver issues, and I made a point of pairing it with a low ABV liqueur rather than anything hard.

1 ounce coconut milk

1 ounce prepared kava liquid (follow directions on the package)

½ ounce amaretto

4 dashes chocolate bitters

Shake all the ingredients in a shaker with ice, then strain into a Collins glass filled with fresh ice.

THINKING Girl's NOTE

The sweet liqueur masks the taste of the herb better in this cocktail than in the mocktails, which is another reason Brittini and I decided to bite the bullet and offer a single kava-alcohol concoction out of the three drinks included here.

Milkshake *Shot*

Cute isn't the word often used to describe a shot, but that's exactly what this little glass of yumminess is. It's compact, it's got a nice beigy melted-ice-cream color, and it's just creamy enough via coconut butter to diminish the bourbon's burn. Using vanilla bean and extract in the syrup helps with that ice cream vibe, and the coconut butter provides a smooth richness in addition to lauric acid to provide an immunity boost and help destroy harmful bacteria. The small dose of fiber also helps slow the alcohol's sugar effect down, making for less chance of an ice-cream-shot headache.

1 ounce bourbon

¾ ounce vanilla syrup (page 248)

1 tablespoon coconut butter

Whisk all the ingredients together to fully dissolve the coconut butter, then pour into a shot glass.

14-Karat Latte

(MOCKTAIL)

Sometimes it's good to remember that we are all worth our weight in gold. More of a tonic or an elixir than a standard mocktail, this beverage is here to remind you of that! Chamomile tea soothes your senses, turmeric eases inflammation, coconut butter makes everything creamy and filling, vanilla provides a cozy baked-goods feeling, and ginger gives it all a little zing ... and all that before we even get to the He Shou Wu, a Chinese herb used for antiaging. He Shou Wu is known for reversing gray hair, and I can say with gusto that it actually does that; my own gray patch is about half the size it was years before I began consuming the herb! It's also great for sexual vitality and restoring the adrenals.

6 ounces strongly brewed hot chamomile tea

1 ounce ginger syrup (page 249)

1 tablespoon coconut butter

1 tablespoon grated turmeric

½ teaspoon vanilla extract

½ teaspoon He Shou Wu powder

1 turmeric slice, for garnish

Blend all the ingredients in a high-powered blender until smooth, then pour into a glass or a coffee mug.

Garnish with the turmeric slice on the edge of the mug.

As with maca, I like the Longevity Power brand for the He Shou Wu, because it's a strongly concentrated extract rather than a fibrous powder, and bloating is always better avoided.

THINKING Girl's NOTE

Spa Day (MOCKTAIL)

If there's one perfect "morning after" mocktail in this book, Spa Day is it. Coconut water hydrates, lime juice detoxes, lavender provides a mood lifter to compensate for the lack of serotonin, and sparkling water gives a little boost of minerals. Equally as sweet as it is tart, and incredibly easy going down, it's the epitome of chill-out beverages. Of course you could also enjoy it in lieu of a cocktail, when you're already feeling good! While I'm not a fan of the term "shake and dump," as it's called in the bar industry when you repurpose the ice used to shake liquids directly into the drink, I am a fan of saving a step and I love the simplicity here.

4 ounces coconut water

1 ounce fresh lime juice

1 ounce lavender syrup (page 248)

Sparkling mineral water, to fill

1 lavender sprig, for garnish

Shake the coconut water, lime juice, and lavender syrup in a shaker with ice.

Pour directly into a mason jar and add the sparkling water to fill.

Garnish with the lavender sprig.

Walk of *Fame*

We've discussed that the carbon dioxide in champagne leads you to feel drunker faster and, thus, hungover quicker. I added fresh coconut water to champagne to help; the result is heavenly! Since coconut water is sweet, you should definitely stick with a Brut/dry bubbly. Brittini and I decided that these two ingredients were a bit lacking in oomph, so we added the aphrodisiacal Damiana. The result? An exquisitely feminine cocktail with a highly unusual flavor and a super-high fun factor. This would be a supreme beverage to serve a tray of at a party, especially for something like a wedding or baby shower. Damiana is surprisingly underused, if not completely unknown, in the cocktail industry. This liqueur was new to Brittini, who was intrigued by its earthiness. The root it's made from adds excellent deep notes without overpowering a drink's flavor.

1 ounce Damiana

2 ounces coconut water

4 ounces Brut champagne

In a champagne flute, add the Damiana, the coconut water, and then the champagne.

This couldn't be a newfangled healthful cocktail book if I didn't delve deep into fat-washing booze and why you absolutely need to do it for the sake of deliciousness. It is, I kid you not, one of the most scrumptious uses of hard alcohol possible. The rich mouth-feel you impart with fat washing makes any drink go down smoother, so watch out for your consumption speed with these drinks and advise your friends to do the same!

When you fat-wash alcohol, you don't end up with much of the original fat, so we won't be overconsuming solid fat by any means. Cocoa butter has great health benefits like reducing wrinkles and preventing baldness. Fat-washing spirits with cocoa butter creates a white chocolate essence, so that's the flavor we played off of for the bourbon drinks.

On the other side of the spectrum, Brittini and I fat-washed vodka with coconut oil, the benefits of which I reviewed in the coconut chapter (page 120), and the result of that was just like Malibu rum, without the sweetness. We were shocked at how much coconut flavor was imparted! The cocoa butter bourbon is mild in comparison. You are, as always, free to switch things up and try cocoa butter in vodka, or coconut oil in bourbon, or bacon fat in tequila, et cetera. To learn how to fat-wash your alcohol for the recipes used in this chapter, see page 140.

How to Fat-Wash Alcohol

This recipe may be scaled down or up as desired.

1 cup coconut oil, cocoa butter, butter, or other fat that is solid at room temperature

2 cups hard alcohol such as vodka, bourbon, or tequila

Melt the room-temperature solid fat over low heat. Allow it to cool slightly.

Pour it into a mixing bowl and add the hard alcohol to it. Stir vigorously.

Pour the mixture into a widemouthed jar, such as a mason jar, and shake occasionally, with the lid on, for 1 hour.

Refrigerate for at least 8 hours, and up to 2 days, shaking every 8 hours or so.

Scoop the hardened fat off the top of the alcohol, then pour it through a strainer into a glass bottle or mason jar. It will keep indefinitely in the refrigerator.

Cupid's Kiss

Smile, it's chocolate and champagne at the door! Surely if Valentine Moonshine (page 151) wasn't the appropriate Valentine's Day–themed drink for you, this one will work out instead. The prosecco lightens an otherwise intensely fruity beverage full of raspberries, which are a plant-based source of omega-3 fatty acids. Crème Yvette is sweetened with honey rather than sugar, which is quite unusual for a liqueur, and contains raspberries, along with several other fruits and violet flower petals. Since it's on the syrupy-sweet side, the tartness of the raspberries provides balance and the cocoa-butter-washed bourbon adds just a hint of cacao.

12 raspberries, plus 3 for garnish

1½ ounces cocoa-butter-washed bourbon (facing page)

½ ounce Crème Yvette

Prosecco, to fill

Shake the 12 raspberries, bourbon, and Crème Yvette in a shaker with ice until the raspberries are broken down.

Strain into a champagne saucer, add the prosecco to fill, and garnish with the remaining raspberries.

Sangria Sunshine

The fun of sangria is that as the fruit sits and absorbs the alcohol, the drink itself grows in flavor. That means it's a very easy punch to whip up a batch hours before friends come over. By the time they arrive, the boozy fruit is as much of a treat as the drink itself! You can use practically any fruit you have on hand; it's one of those concoctions you can't really go wrong with. The recipe here is for a single serving, so just multiply it as needed to make a big batch. If refrigerated, it will keep for about 24 hours before the fruit begins to break down too much to be enjoyable any longer.

3 ounces red wine

2 ounces fresh orange juice

1½ ounces cocoa-butter-washed bourbon (page 140)

½ ounce fresh lemon juice

¼ ounce vanilla syrup (page 248)

6 raspberries

3 apple slices

2 orange slices

Add all the ingredients in a mason jar and stir to combine.

Let it sit for several minutes or up to several hours. When ready to serve, fill the mason jar with ice cubes.

Creamsicle Pop-Up

If a screwdriver (the drink, not the tool) and a creamsicle had a baby, this cocktail would be the offspring. It's simple like a screwdriver, with the prominent flavor of orange and the back notes of vodka, and it has a desserty vanilla vibe from the home-made vanilla syrup and a lush rich-ness from the coconut-oil-washed vodka. A drop of bitter orange oil will lift your mood as it amplifies the orange aspect. Variations on soda fountain drinks are some of the most nostalgic and fun drinks to make, and they are still gaining in popularity in bars due to the fact that they're often more complex. This drink is a fairly simple version and easy to make at home. Without the coconut-oil wash, the smoothness would be lost.

2 ounces coconut-oil-washed vodka (page 140)

1 ounce fresh orange juice

¼ ounce vanilla syrup (page 248)

1 tablespoon orange zest

1 drop food-grade bitter orange oil

Shake all the ingredients in a shaker with ice.

Strain into a highball glass filled with fresh ice.

This cocktail is *way* too easy to drink, so watch your speed!

So-Cal Sipper

To play off of how much the coconut-oil-washed vodka reminds us of Malibu rum without the sweetness, Brittini and I created a juicy beverage with a slight hint of the tropics. Pear juice is easy to find but it's unusual for it to be used in cocktails, which is a shame considering its vitamin K, potassium, and glutathione. It's also great for digestion, as it contains pectin. The flavor of the juice reminds me of my childhood, and pear pairs perfectly with orgeat, the almond-based syrup. With orange bitters, which adds just a touch of extra citrus to the lemon juice, and the rich flavor of the coconut-oil-washed vodka, you'd swear you were drinking a snack.

2 ounces coconut-oil-washed vodka (page 140)

1 ounce fresh pear juice

½ ounce fresh lemon juice

¼ ounce orgeat syrup (page 248)

1 dash orange bitters

1 orange twist, for garnish

Shake all the ingredients (except the garnish) in a shaker with ice.

Strain into a champagne saucer and garnish with the orange twist.

Chocolate York

I didn't think a basic Manhattan could be improved upon! The simple blend of whiskey, vermouth, and bitters is one of my favorite classic cocktails. In this rendition, it is revved up to full city speed via cocoa-butter-washed bourbon. In addition to Angostura, we added chocolate bitters to further play off of the cocoa-butter-enhanced bourbon and swapped out straight vermouth for the more herbaceous Carpano. Chocolate bitters is a natural match to cocoa butter as they originate from the same source. It brings out the flavor of the washed bourbon as well. The result is masculine enough to still be considered a manly Manhattan, yet it has been feminized enough to be a drink that is a lot smoother!

2 ounces cocoa-butter-washed bourbon (page 140)

¾ ounce Carpano Antica

4 dashes chocolate bitters

1 light dash Angostura bitters

1 Luxardo cherry, for garnish

Stir all the ingredients (except the garnish) in a mixing glass with ice and strain into a champagne saucer.

Garnish with the Luxardo cherry.

Liquid Chocolate Orange

Do you know those candy orbs of chocolate that are designed to be lightly banged on, so as to break into segments like an orange? They have just a hint of orange essence, making the chocolate all the more irresistible. This drink tastes like that in liquid form! Campari can be acquired in a version that does not contain artificial colors, but the flavor and texture will be a little different. The U.S.-made alternative that came out recently is by Leopold Bros., the company that makes the Alpine herbal liqueur used throughout this book. They employ cochineal for color, aka bug juice, so it isn't an option for vegans. They don't use glycerin or glycol, which gives liqueurs their viscous nature, so it has a lighter mouth-feel than Campari.

1½ ounces cocoa-butter-washed bourbon (page 140)

¾ ounce Carpano Antica

1 ounce Campari

1 orange peel, for garnish

Stir the bourbon, Carpano, and Campari in a mixing glass with ice.

Strain into a rocks glass with a single large ice cube and garnish with the orange peel.

White Chocolate Soda

Sidle up to the soda fountain for this dreamy drink! You can scarcely tell it contains any booze because it's so very smooth, so watch out for how many of these you knock back because it is still ABV-packed. Crème de cacao imparts the chocolate flavor and vanilla syrup adds the dessert quality. At one time vanilla was used medicinally far more than it's used now, and it's long been considered an aphrodisiac, a stress reducer, and a combatant of inflammation. It's even useful for cognitive enhancement! Sparkling mineral water contains healthful minerals such as magnesium, but make sure that you aren't buying a brand that has a high sodium content; that would negate its hydrating effect and worsen any issues caused by drinking alcohol.

2 ounces coconut-oil-washed vodka (page 140)

¼ ounce vanilla syrup (page 248)

½ ounce crème de cacao

Sparkling mineral water, to fill

Add the vodka, vanilla syrup, and crème de cacao to a highball glass.

Fill the glass with ice and stir, then top with the sparkling water.

Valentine Moonshine

Have you ever wished you could drink a glass of Valentine's Day? If so, hello and welcome to your own personal heaven! Chocolate, cherry, floral, bitter, and sweet, this cocktail plays on the chocolate hints of cocoa-butter-washed bourbon with a whole lot of extra love added. Hibiscus is used as an aid for the liver, making the liqueur a solid antidote to, well, itself. Luxardo cherry juice is the syrup in which the cherries are packed. While they contain sugar, they are still a million times more natural—and far better-tasting—than maraschino cherries. If you want to be more healthful than that, thaw some frozen cherries and use the juice from them instead, along with a dash of noncaloric natural sweetener.

2 ounces cocoa-butter-washed bourbon (page 140)

1 ounce hibiscus liqueur

¼ ounce Luxardo cherry juice

2 dashes chocolate bitters

Berry sparkling water, to fill

Shake all the ingredients except the sparkling water in a shaker with ice.

Pour into a double old-fashioned glass filled with fresh ice and top with the berry sparkling water.

THINKING Girl's NOTE

You could use plain sparkling water instead of the berry, but I love the way it acts as the icing on the Valentine's Day cake.

The health values of hard spices are manifold, and their flavors should rightfully extend far beyond the holiday season that they're typically confined to. Clove is antifungal and provides relief for oral pain, nutmeg reduces insomnia, and black pepper helps you to better absorb the nutrients of whatever else you consume, just to name a few benefits.

This chapter features simple pantry staples that last for years, can be grated on the fly, and look supercool left whole in drinks. They are accoutrements à la Martha Stewart, only completely attainable and simple! It does take some focused creating to ensure that the cocktails made with hard spices don't taste generically like the holidays; if you combine too many spices at once, the likelihood is that the drink will end up with a gingerbread flavor and lose all individual notes. Because of that, care has been taken to use just one or two spices for many of these drinks, lest you feel like you're drinking a Christmas potpourri candle.

Spiced Maria

Like everything about a Bloody Mary except for the tomato juice? Welcome, then, to your new love! A spicy, southwestern version of a Bloody Maria, this drink swaps out tomato juice for carrot juice, hot sauce for smoky chipotle powder, and horseradish for cumin seed powder. It has a similar vibe to the classic, but it's sweeter, smokier, brighter, and all around a little more fun. Cumin has a nutty, peppery flavor, lots of iron, and the ability to enhance your liver's production of detox enzymes, which is way helpful when consuming alcohol. Chipotle is smoked jalapeño and will rev up your metabolism with its charred heat.

4 ounces fresh or bottled carrot juice

2 ounces tequila

½ ounce fresh lemon juice

2 dashes celery bitters

2 shakes cumin seed powder

1 shake chipotle powder

Shake all the ingredients in a shaker with ice.

Strain into a highball glass filled with fresh ice.

Smooth as Suede

Both the color and vibe of this drink reminds me exactly of a beautiful vintage leather purse. Nutmeg has been used for eons in Chinese and Indian traditional medicines for helping with everything from tooth pain to indigestion. It goes well with both sweet and savory flavors; in the sweet sense, it's the main flavor of eggnog and on the savory side it's a common addition to macaroni and cheese. Here, we play up its ability to pair with sweet Benedictine, a scotch-based liqueur made of twenty-seven assorted plants and spices. It contains hyssop, a herb used for anti-aging and lowering blood sugar, as well as lemon balm, which helps calm menstrual cramps and ease PMS.

2 ounces scotch

½ ounce Benedictine

1 tablespoon orange zest

6 grinds nutmeg, plus 6 for garnish

1 orange peel, for garnish

Stir the scotch, Benedictine, orange zest, and 6 grinds nutmeg together in a mixing glass with ice.

Strain into a rocks glass with a single large ice cube and sprinkle the additional nutmeg on top.

Express the orange peel over the entire glass.

THINKING Girl's NOTE

Similar to that of Chartreuse, very few people know the full recipe for Benedictine.

Licorice Sticks

Sambuca is back for an encore, only now without coffee to mellow down its anise quality. This cocktail is like a more grown-up version of the White Chocolate Soda (page 150) in the fat-washed chapter; it's equally easy to make and tastes like it has much less alcohol than it does. Here, we cut the sweetness of the sambuca a little with a drop of food-grade black pepper oil. Fun fact: Black pepper oil has been scientifically proven to help people quit smoking! Not only does it alleviate cravings for cigarettes, it also lessens the withdrawal symptoms caused by quitting. Outside of that, it's mentally stimulating and it reduces anxiety.

2 ounces sambuca

1 drop food–grade black pepper oil

Sparkling mineral water, to fill

Add the sambuca and pepper oil to a highball glass, then fill it with ice and stir.

Add the sparkling water to top.

Black pepper oil is potent, so one drop should do you plenty to add a touch of warmth.

THINKING *Girl's* NOTE

159

Beach Day

This is the perfect cocktail to toss in a thermos and hit the sandy shore! Cardamom might be unexpected with gin, pineapple, and lime, but it adds a charming, sweet quality—as well as the ability to aid with nausea and bloating, eliminate waste through the kidneys, and lower blood pressure. Pineapple juice contains bromelain, which is used medicinally for a host of things, from reducing hay fever to relaxing muscles to helping the body shed fat. The bromelain is most concentrated in the stem, so enjoy a snack of those separately!

1 cardamom pod

½ ounce fresh lime juice

2 ounces London Dry gin

2 ounces fresh pineapple juice

1 lime wheel, for garnish

Muddle the cardamom pod with the lime juice in a shaker.

Add the gin and pineapple juice to the muddled lime juice, then add ice and shake.

Strain into a Collins glass filled with fresh ice and garnish with the lime wheel.

Brunch Punch

Hey, Pedro, so nice to see you again! The sweet and silky sherry we love gets a shot of blood orange juice to sour it up, along with mulling spices for a punch that would be excellent batched up to serve a Thanksgiving crowd. Mulling spices contain orange peel, which rounds out the orange juice, as well as cinnamon, nutmeg, and allspice. Allspice improves blood circulation, is great for oral health, and provides relief from arthritis. I chose the mulling spices combo, rather than a single spice, for this drink because I felt the orange juice and wine stood up well to multiple spices, and because mulling spices are so easy to find and have on hand. This drink basically screams "holiday party!"

1 tablespoon mulling spices

2 ounces Pedro Ximénez

2 ounces fresh blood orange juice

Sparkling mineral water, to fill

Steep the mulling spices in 2 tablespoons of hot water for about 5 minutes, then strain.

Add the Pedro Ximénez, blood orange juice, and strained mulling spice liquid into a highball glass and stir with ice.

Add the sparkling water to top.

Bathing in Gold

Hot cider is a good thing, which makes hot cider with yummy herbal liqueur and pumpkin pie spices a great thing. The quantity of spices may seem like a lot, but it takes a good amount to cut through the sweetness of the cider and the liqueur. Pumpkin pie spice is a blend of ground cinnamon, cloves, allspice, ginger, and nutmeg, and is an outrageously popular fall flavor. Often erroneously referred to as "pumpkin spice," most beverages and desserts that are so labeled typically only contain the pie spice mix and not any actual pumpkin flavorings. At a bar, a drink like this would likely be made with a similar amount of spice, making the flavor a potentially familiar one. The mélange of spices is anti-inflammatory, full of antioxidants, and excellent for digestion.

7 ounces apple cider

2 teaspoons pumpkin pie spice

2½ ounces Leopold Bros. Three Pins Alpine Herbal Liqueur

Heat the apple cider with the pumpkin pie spice in a small pot on low heat, stirring to combine.

Pour into a coffee mug and add the liqueur.

Mai Chai (MOCKTAIL)

Chai is a tea beverage that people usually think is much more work to make than it actually is. In reality, all you have to do is boil black tea with some hard spices, strain, sweeten to taste, and add a milk of your choosing. I love toffee stevia in this because of the candylike flavor it brings to the sugar-free table, and I think it goes nicely with cinnamon and cardamom. Your black tea choice can be anything from oolong to English Breakfast; thankfully all black teas are full of antioxidants called theaflavins, which can help prevent cancer and strokes. Since tea is sprayed with large amounts of pesticides, organic is the wise option to ensure that you get its benefits and not a piping-hot cup of toxic chemicals.

1 tea bag of a strong black tea

1 cinnamon stick

1 cardamom pod

2 peppercorns

1 dropperful toffee stevia

2 ounces coconut milk (or other milk of your choice)

Steep the tea bag, cinnamon stick, cardamom pod, and peppercorns in a mug of hot water for 5 minutes.

Strain, then add the toffee stevia and milk.

Healed Mary

(MOCKTAIL)

Some time after poor Mary got all bloodied, I imagine she took a break from being a hangover brunch cocktail and decided to heal herself with a moment of purity. In this spirit I've created a mocktail with Bloody Mary flavors and with a fresh ingredient focus. Is such a thing possible? you may ask. I'd love to think so! With simple ingredients such as cayenne pepper in lieu of hot sauce and fresh horseradish instead of jarred, this mocktail is even more healthful than a glass of tomato juice. Lemon juice adds tartness and some detox, cayenne and black pepper will calm inflammation and speed up your metabolism, and the tomato juice fills you with lycopene, the beautiful biochemical in tomatoes that is more bio-available when they are cooked than raw.

6 ounces tomato juice

½ ounce fresh lemon juice

1 tablespoon grated horseradish

2 shakes cayenne pepper

2 grinds black pepper

Add all the ingredients to a highball glass and stir.

Fill the glass with ice.

I felt that green juice was requisite to include in *The Thinking Girl's Guide to Drinking* because it has gained such mainstream traction in recent years. Not only are there juice bars popping up in small towns everywhere, but bars in major cities often include green juice in at least one of their cocktails.

Personally, my family juiced veggies throughout my childhood. My father actually turned orange once from too much carrot juice! When I first experienced health issues, juice cleanses were my initial go-to. I don't generally recommend them nowadays because they're so extreme, but juice does have value by way of the nutrients being bio-available (aka very easy to absorb).

To many in the mainstream, the idea that you can drink your veggies is still pretty revolutionary; it's certainly something I encourage as a supplement for the sake of getting extra vitamins and nutrients. It's also surprisingly easy to use assorted green juices in cocktails. I was initially concerned they'd taste like salad no matter what else we added to them, but thank goodness I was quite wrong! These drinks add some unique nutrients into your diet that a cocktail would generally never contain.

Celebratini

Celebrate your celebrity sensibility—or acquire it, if you don't have any already!—with this sinfully sippable martini. Celery juice hydrates and brings in phosphorous and folic acid, while apple juice lends a little hint of sweetness along with a potential reduction of asthma symptoms and cancer prevention. Celery bitters is key to enhancing the celery juice's flavor, and it doesn't take much to make a big difference with it. Since the quantities of juice in this are small, so as to leave room for the ever-important standards of vodka and vermouth, this is a good choice for batching up for something like a Hollywood awards show night.

1½ ounces celery juice

1½ ounces vodka

½ ounce apple juice

½ ounce dry Italian vermouth

1 large dash celery bitters

1 celery frond, for garnish

Stir all the ingredients (except the garnish) in a mixing glass with ice and strain into a martini glass.

Garnish with the celery frond.

Springtime Getaway

For all its glorious magenta color, dragon fruit, also known as pitaya, is quite mild in flavor. It jazzes up this light and lovely bevvie with its pink hue, polyunsaturated fatty acids, and multiple B vitamins. Celery juice also contains multiple B vitamins, along with folic acid and potassium, and is also light in color, so it doesn't turn the drink murky. Brittini was pleased and surprised with the beauty we were able to attain here. With lemon juice for a hint of tartness, lavender syrup for some floral sweetness, and aquavit for herbal tones, this cocktail is very refreshing and will add spring to your day or night no matter what the season!

1½ ounces frozen dragon fruit purée

1½ ounces aquavit

1 ounce fresh celery juice (homemade or purchased from a juice bar)

1 ounce lavender syrup (page 248)

½ ounce fresh lemon juice

Dissolve the dragon fruit purée in 2 tablespoons of hot water.

Shake all the ingredients in a shaker with ice.

Strain over fresh ice in a Collins glass.

Forest Jade

You'd never guess by drinking this cocktail that it has more cucumber juice in it than any other ingredient. Cucumber juice is a common base for green juices because you get so much liquid out of the intensely hydrating vegetable and it has a mild, pleasant taste that, while distinctly vegetal, isn't at all serious like kale or spinach. If you're feeling spendy, you can pass on the vodka for a full two-ounce pour of Chartreuse; the taste will be even lovelier, but it will raise the price tag a little bit because you'll plow through the bottle quicker. There isn't a sweetener added here due to the inherent sweetness of Chartreuse, which the detoxifying lime juice won't cut through excessively.

3 ounces fresh cucumber juice

1 ounce Chartreuse

1 ounce vodka

½ ounce fresh lime juice

2 dashes celery bitters

Pour all the ingredients into a highball glass, then fill with ice and stir.

Summer Smash

Have you ever gotten that prickly, burning feeling on your tongue from eating pineapple? It happened to me as a child and I assumed I was allergic, which turned out to be incorrect. That feeling is actually caused by the pineapple's bromelain enzyme, which aids digestion and tenderizes meat. The pieces of pineapple in this summery cocktail are not only delicious to eat if they don't bother your tongue, but the fiber in them will also help slow the absorption of alcohol into your bloodstream. While fresh pineapple is excellent if available, frozen is perfectly fine and the cocktail will be just as lively. Cucumber plays a prevalent role as the highest volume liquid, but the pineapple is flavorful enough to overshadow it and keep things feeling fruity.

1 cup pineapple chunks, plus one wedge for garnish

½ ounce fresh lime juice

3 ounces fresh cucumber juice

1 ounce fresh pineapple juice

1½ ounces white rum

1 cucumber slice, for garnish

Muddle the pineapple with the lime juice in a shaker.

Add ice, the juices, and rum and shake.

Pour directly into a highball glass and garnish with the pineapple wedge and cucumber slice.

There's enough pineapple here that no sweetener is necessary, but if you want it a tad sweeter, you can add a dash of the juice that leaks out while you are slicing the pineapple.

THINKING *Girl's* NOTE

Green Goddess

It felt important to include some drinks that called for mixed green juice because I know that's something you can find in a mainstream grocery store pretty much anywhere now. Typically, a mixed green juice will contain apples, cucumber, celery, and some leafy greens like spinach and/or kale. If you can get one without apple juice, that's the healthier option, and a better choice presuming you won't miss the fruitiness. If you prefer green juice with apples, you'll still reap the benefits of the other ingredients, and there are far worse things to drink than apple juice! This simple cocktail is herbaceous from the Leopold Bros. liqueur and is fun to drink out of a champagne saucer.

2 ounces mixed green juice

2 ounces Leopold Bros. Three Pins Alpine Herbal Liqueur

1 basil leaf and 1 lemon wheel, for garnish

Shake the green juice and liqueur in a shaker with ice and strain into a champagne saucer.

Garnish with the basil leaf and lemon wheel.

Raw Sienna

When Brittini read my proposed recipe for this drink, she wasn't particularly thrilled about the potential color it would create. I knew the color would turn out to be a murky brown, but thankfully it tastes every bit as good as I imagined it would. I usually recommend using Cynar 70, but in this drink it was too strong, since celery juice and apple juice hold less weight than heavy artichoke leaf liqueur. The sparkling water lightens the color a bit, but it still errs on the murky side. Embrace your own interesting colors with this vitamin-packed cocktail!

2 ounces fresh celery juice

2 ounces fresh apple juice

2 ounces Cynar

Sparkling mineral water, to fill

Pour the juices and Cynar into a mason jar, stir, and fill with ice.

Top with the sparkling water.

Green Juice Splash (MOCKTAIL)

Parsley may not be a normal mocktail ingredient, but it is a healthful and delicious one. The leaves are muddled to impart their flavor, then strained out so that your drink doesn't resemble a food garnish. Parsley controls blood pressure, supports kidney function, relieves bloating and nausea, and strengthens the immune system. Odd fact: Ancient Greeks and Romans would not eat the stuff, but according to folklore, Romans wore it as crowns to ward off intoxication. If you're feeling like death warmed over yourself today, this mocktail is a perfect antidote. Green juice will also, of course, help with detoxification, and sparkling water will add some much needed minerals. If all is well, even better! Make like the opposite of an ancient Greek and enjoy.

2 stems parsley leaves

Sparkling mineral water, to fill, divided

5 ounces mixed green juice

Muddle the parsley leaves with a splash of sparkling water in a shaker.

Add the green juice and ice and shake.

Strain into a highball glass filled with fresh ice and top with more sparkling water.

Sober Summer Smash (MOCKTAIL)

Similar to Summer Smash (page 177) earlier in this chapter, this mocktail is an alcohol-free version that is equally full of juicy pineapple pieces. Minus the rum, it's every bit as replete with sunshine as the alcoholic version. In the place of rum we doubled the cucumber juice, making the drink all the better for you. Cucumber juice, apple juice, and celery juice are the most oft-used fresh juices in bars nowadays. Similar to the alcoholic version, you can use fresh or frozen pineapple; this drink will work perfectly with frozen if you do not have fresh on hand. The drink also doubles as a digestion-enhancing snack with its full cup of pineapple.

1 cup fresh or frozen pineapple chunks, plus one wedge for garnish

½ ounce fresh lime juice

6 ounces fresh cucumber juice

1 ounce fresh pineapple juice

1 cucumber slice, for garnish

Muddle the pineapple with lime juice in a shaker.

Add ice and the juices and shake.

Pour directly into a highball glass and garnish with the pineapple wedge and cucumber slice.

Choco-LOVE

Cacao is queen for that theobromine high, even though it isn't the only food that contains theobromine. Side note: Try Macambo seeds sometime! They're in the same family as cacao beans and also high in theobromine. You eat them like nuts, and they're one of my favorite snacks because they are crunchy and creamy.

In this chapter, we'll melt chocolate, use both baking cocoa powder and raw cacao powder, and we will *definitely* avoid commercial Godiva liqueur. Good-quality cacao products are far more of a health food than they're given credit for! From containing many B vitamins to PMS-relieving magnesium, this food is more a medicine than it is a vice, as long as you eat a health-promoting version.

Organic is as important here as it is with coffee, since cacao plants are also heavily pesticide-ridden. Fair trade is even more important than organic, in my opinion, because who wants to eat or drink slave labor?! You'll taste the difference in higher-quality cacao products, and both your taste buds and your conscience will thank you.

Tiger's Eye

The chocolate and orange-marriage was so successful in Liquid Chocolate Orange (page 148) that we decided to bring it back for more. Cointreau and orange bitters bring the citrus to the table, standard roasted cocoa powder makes everything taste like chocolate, and vodka provides a neutral backdrop. If you haven't tried flaming an orange peel before, it's worth the initial scare of doing it! The sizzling of volatile oils makes such an amazingly scrumptious, over-the-top burnt-orange flavor that you'll continue to get the aroma of it as you sip the drink.

2 ounces vodka

½ ounce Cointreau

1 tablespoon orange zest

1 teaspoon cocoa powder

1 dash orange bitters

1 orange peel, for garnish

Shake all the ingredients except the orange peel in a shaker with ice.

Strain into a champagne saucer and, if desired, flame the orange peel over the top.

Tiger's Eye stones help you release anxieties and fears, so I thought I'd add some of that metaphoric energy to this cocktail, since the flavors reminded me of the crystal's gold and dark hues.

THINKING Girl's NOTE

Shiny Copper Penny

This drink was named for the luscious golden-brown color imparted in it by raw cacao powder, which is much lighter and brighter than standard baking cocoa. Since it isn't roasted, raw cacao retains more of its inherent antioxidants, which can get destroyed by heat processing. It also tends to have a potent effect, so if you are sensitive to caffeine or to the "feel good" effects of chocolate (which come from the theobromine), you will probably react more strongly to raw cacao products than you do to the standard processed ones. With some bourbon, vanilla, and chocolate additions, this drink is like a dairy-free iced boozy hot chocolate.

2 ounces bourbon

½ ounce vanilla syrup (page 248)

½ tablespoon raw cacao powder

½ teaspoon chocolate extract

4 dashes chocolate bitters

Shake all the ingredients in a shaker with ice.

Strain into a rocks glass filled with fresh ice.

Any Port in a Storm

Tawny port is the more aged version of port and is slightly reminiscent of sherry; ruby is the more juicy, red, less aged one. For a cocoa powder and port combo, I like the tawny better, but you could for sure try this with the ruby if you wanted a more fruity drink. Roasted cocoa powder, though not the antioxidant behemoth that raw cacao powder is, still retains many excellent health benefits. The flavonoids in cocoa help to reduce systemic inflammation and relax the muscles in your blood vessels, thus improving blood flow. Cocoa powder has no inherent sweetness, but port has plenty. Just a little cocoa adds a strong chocolate flavor without any additional sugar.

½ tablespoon cocoa powder

3 ounces tawny port, divided

Dissolve the cocoa powder in ½ ounce tawny port in a sherry glass, then add the remaining port and stir.

Tawny port has more of an "adult" taste than ruby port generally does, which is the opposite of something people would generally say about a chocolate beverage!

THINKING
Girl's
NOTE

Lady Slipper

Just when you thought Pedro Ximénez couldn't get any more delicious, we went and chocolated it up with some crème de cacao and chocolate extract. Chocolate extract is a godsend of an ingredient, being composed of nothing but cacao beans and alcohol—similar to how vanilla extract is just vanilla beans plus alcohol—and it can up the chocolate factor of anything you add it to without you having to use any actual chocolate. No lie, I actually took a break from writing this headnote because a lightbulb went off in my head; I realized what I should do with a less-than-top-shelf bottle of vodka someone brought to a barbecue at my home. In about two minutes, I made chocolate extract by throwing a cup of cacao nibs and a couple cups of vodka into an old mason jar. It'll be a few months before it's ready, but when it is, I'll have everyone reading this to thank for the inspiration!

3 ounces Pedro Ximénez

¼ ounce crème de cacao

½ teaspoon chocolate extract

Pour all the ingredients into a sherry glass and stir.

Call Me Frida

An artist friend of mine is curating a collection entitled "Letters to Frida" in which she asked different writers and musicians to write a letter to Frida Kahlo. She asked me to take part and I wrote a poem about how I would host a dinner party for the artist. The project was running through my mind when I came up with this cocktail, so I decided to name it after her. Guajillo chocolate is a Mexican chocolate that has chili in it and is every bit as spicy as you might imagine. It has a unique texture and a heavenly taste; the Taza brand is organic, ground by hand, fair trade, and—best yet—available throughout the United States.

2 ounces tequila

½ ounce pure maple syrup

1 teaspoon grated guajillo chocolate, plus extra for garnish

4 dashes chocolate chili bitters

Pour all the ingredients into a rocks glass and stir.

Add a large cube of ice and grate additional chocolate over the top.

Flowers and Chocolate

The name pretty much says it all—this cocktail tastes like flowers and chocolate! The chocolate flavor comes by way of both extract and bitters, the flowers are evoked with fresh lavender syrup, falernum rounds out the sweetness with notes of almond and ginger, and spiced rum jazzes it all up just enough to cut through the assorted sweet tastes. Spiced rum doesn't have to be sugary; good-quality organic ones will add only a minimal amount of additional sweetener, so I definitely recommend using one of those. Mainstream brands, such as those seen in TV commercials, tend to have so much added sweetener that they can no longer even be categorized as a rum in Europe! They're called "rum-based spirits" instead. If all you can find, though, is a sweeter variety, reduce the amount of syrup or falernum.

2 ounces spiced rum

¾ ounce lavender syrup (page 248)

½ ounce falernum

¼ teaspoon chocolate extract

3 dashes chocolate bitters

Stir all the ingredients in a double old-fashioned glass and add one large ice cube.

Mocking Mocha (MOCKTAIL)

Confession: I've spent over half of my adult life not drinking coffee. I've always loved the taste of coffee but was hesitant to have it be a part of my daily life, whether because I had one chronic illness or another chronic illness, or because I was too control freak-ish to be accepting of a substance being necessary to get my day going. A year or two ago I said "F that" and got back on the magic juice on the daily, with every plan to never get back off it again because, hello, it's crazy good. For many, coffee isn't an option—some don't like the taste, some can't handle the caffeine, and some find it too acidic. For all of those people, there are delicious coffee-substitute teas made of dandelion root, chicory, and/or carob. Whether you're a coffee lover or not, this mocktail is a festive way to not indulge in any potential café-au-regret.

3 tablespoons cocoa powder

8 ounces strongly brewed coffee substitute (such as chicory or dandelion-root tea), divided

3 tablespoons cocoa powder

4 ounces coconut milk

2 ounces vanilla syrup (page 248)

Dissolve the cocoa powder in 1 ounce coffee substitute in a large mug.

Add the remaining ingredients and stir.

Armored Hot Chocolate

(KAVA MOCKTAIL)

There is a lot happening in this drink. Before we get into the kava part, this is my version of a BULLETPROOF® Coffee, only with hot chocolate instead of coffee. That means it contains grass-fed butter for inflammation reduction and MCT oil for fat-burning and antimicrobial properties. When making this drink style, hot liquid is blended with fats so that they get emulsified and thus come out creamy. I took things one step further here by adding the increasingly popular herb kava, which is a nonalcoholic, mildly mind-altering substance. Depending on the type you get, the effects can be more stimulating or relaxing. No matter which type you try, the herb numbs your entire mouth and it feels crazy weird for ten to twenty minutes. Kava has a strong, bitter taste that this drink covers up as well as anything could.

8 ounces hot water

2 tablespoons raw cacao powder

2 tablespoons butter (I prefer salted)

1 tablespoon MCT oil

1 tablespoon instant kava powder

2 droppers-full toffee stevia

Blend all the ingredients in a blender on high for 3 to 5 minutes, then pour into a coffee mug.

Because of the fat content, drink this alone, not with a meal, so that it has fat-burning effects rather than fat-hoarding ones.

THINKING
Girl's
NOTE

To keep tummies content, mint is a safe and satisfying choice. When picturing mint's usage in cocktails, people typically think of either heavily sweetened schnapps or Irish Spring soap–colored Grasshopper drinks that taste like something between toothpaste and cheap ice cream. There's no need to head in that direction!

Fresh mint, peppermint extract, and mint teas are all featured in this chapter to bring you refreshing brightness, not cloying sweetness or reminders of your dental cleaning. Mint is already a common ingredient in drinks, being a staple in juleps, mojitos, and more, but it is generally only used muddled fresh. By making mint tea, the flavors become concentrated, and become even more so by using extract.

We'll also coax out more flavors than you may be accustomed to. Have you ever wondered why fresh mint tastes so different from mint-flavored items? The reason for this is because fresh mint sold in groceries is generally spearmint, whereas mint used for mint flavor is typically peppermint. Fresh peppermint is a huge treat; you can grow your own in a small pot and it can be found occasionally at farmer's markets or as a plant at stores like Trader Joe's. Whenever I call for mint leaves, if you can get peppermint fresh, please do replace the spearmint with them!

Mango-jito

I loved the idea of a mango and mint pairing, but I was a little concerned about how well they'd go together. The lime juice ended up acting as an integral factor in melding them into a beautiful, perfect harmony—this cocktail is mojitolicious! You can use fresh or frozen mango here; the drink is strained, so if frozen mango thaws into soggy fruit, no worries! It's the flavor and the juice we're after, anyway. Being yellow in color, mangoes contain lutein, which is good for eye health. Perfect for a summer's day, or any day you want to turn into a summer's day, a mango-jito is a minty, fruity glass of joy.

3 ounces mango chunks, fresh or frozen (with juice, if any has accumulated)

8 fresh mint leaves, plus 1 sprig for garnish

½ ounce fresh lime juice

2 ounces white rum

Muddle the mango and mint leaves with the lime juice in a shaker.

Add ice and the rum, then shake.

Strain into a highball glass filled with fresh ice and garnish with the mint sprig.

Fairy Iced Tea

Ah, absinthe. It became legal in America about ten years ago after a long ban based on technicalities of the wormwood ingredient. I have to admit, it was the unusually intoxicating nature of absinthe that finally got me to be okay with, and eventually fall a little bit in love with, the flavor of anise/licorice. Absinthe is superhigh proof, so we used only half a standard pour of it, and because of its herbal components, the high can be a bit different and more intense than regular booze, so consume cautiously.

4 ounces brewed peppermint tea, chilled

1 ounce absinthe

¼ ounce fresh lemon juice

Shake all the ingredients in a shaker with ice and strain into a champagne saucer.

To make peppermint tea yourself, take a couple of sprigs of fresh mint and steep them in a cup of near-boiling water for 5 to 10 minutes. I like to keep the sprigs whole so that I can just pull them right back out of the mug, because #lifehack.

THINKING
Girl's
NOTE

Fairy Tea Soda

Similar to Fairy Iced Tea (page 204), only with a dash of hydration via sparkling mineral water, this cocktail should be treated the same way: gingerly. Peppermint tea mellows out the licorice taste of the "green fairy" alcohol while soothing any potential nausea from consuming a high-proof, herb-filled booze, and lemon juice offers a tiny touch of detoxification as you toxify. While absinthe is not hallucinogenic as some people have claimed, it does indeed make for a different style of buzz than regular liquor. It's been considered more lucid, yet also more dreamlike. This is caused by thujone, the active ingredient in wormwood, the plant from which absinthe is made.

4 ounces brewed peppermint tea, chilled

1 ounce absinthe

¼ ounce fresh lemon juice

Sparkling mineral water, to fill

Shake all the ingredients in a shaker with ice.

Strain into a Collins glass filled with fresh ice and top with sparkling water.

Mintini

It took a few tries to get this recipe to shape up as I'd hoped would be possible. Brittini made some alterations to the original proportions I'd planned and added celery bitters. Before long, we both agreed that a mint martini that wasn't sweet could indeed be a viable drink. Since so many of the drinks in this chapter are sweet, it was important to me to offer a savory option or two, and a martini is always a sound option for one of those! We didn't want it to be overpoweringly minty, just enough of a hint to render it obvious that this particular bevvie had something unusual happening, but feel free to increase the amount of extract. This is a standard take on a martini in terms of vermouth and gin proportions, but with a unique and easy-to-execute twist by way of the mint and bitters.

2 ½ ounces London Dry gin

½ ounce dry Italian vermouth

4 drops peppermint extract

2 dashes celery bitters

Stir all the ingredients in a mixing glass with ice and strain into a martini glass.

Mint Be Jeweled

Coming in second for savory, this version of a mint julep is unsweetened and drinks more like a strong mint tea with lemon than a juicy cocktail. While the addition of brewed mint tea is a small one, it leads to a very different overall taste than that of a standard julep. You don't have to crush ice if it sounds like a pain, but it will definitely add to the experience and authenticity and only takes a couple of minutes! Mint tea can calm nausea as well as a nervous stomach, helping to mellow out this otherwise strong cocktail. Additional mint leaves add the fresh-mint aspect you'd expect from a julep, and between the two, this cocktail is a minty delight.

2 ounces bourbon

1 ounce strongly brewed mint tea, chilled

¾ ounce fresh lemon juice

5 fresh mint leaves, plus 1 sprig for garnish

Fill a julep cup with ice. Transfer the ice to a zip-lock bag and crush it with a mallet or hammer; pour the ice into the julep cup.

Shake all the ingredients except the mint sprig in a shaker with ice.

Strain into the julep cup and garnish with the mint sprig.

Christmas Cocktail

What's red and green and delicious? Christmas may or may not taste good depending on what you eat for the holiday, but this red-and-green drink is a guaranteed winner no matter the season! Since the texture of frozen strawberries is pretty mushy once they're thawed, you'll want to use fresh berries and save this drink for when fresh is available. Strawberry tops are generally discarded, but I encourage you to keep them in the drink and eat them! They reduce bloating and are great for digestion. Lavender syrup adds sweetness and a calming effect without any extra sugar, and rhubarb bitters has a wonderfully unique taste that goes as well with strawberry, as if the two were baked in a pie together.

4 strawberries, plus 1 for garnish

12 fresh mint leaves

¾ ounce fresh lemon juice

2 ounces vodka

½ ounce lavender syrup (page 248)

2 dashes rhubarb bitters

Sparkling mineral water, to fill

Muddle the strawberries and mint with the lemon juice in a shaker.

Add ice, the vodka, lavender syrup, and bitters, then shake.

Pour directly into a mason jar and garnish with the strawberry.

Snow (Mint) White (MOCKTAIL)

This warm and wintry sipper is like a chocolate peppermint mocha, only without the coffee. Instead, the white chocolate is offset by Maca Bliss powder, the über-concentrated fiber-less maca extract previously used in the Sexpresso mocktail (page 117). It adds a malty quality in addition to great adaptogenic properties that will help your body deal with stress better. Peppermint extract can be substituted with a drop or two of food-grade peppermint essential oil if preferred; the flavors are inter-changeable. I love how peppermint extract has such a cooling effect on a hot drink, making it invigorating as it freshens breath and even goes so far as to kill some of the microbes that cause bad breath in the first place!

1½ ounces white chocolate

6 ounces coconut milk

1 teaspoon Longevity Power Maca Bliss powder

¼ teaspoon peppermint extract

In a saucepan, melt the white chocolate with the coconut milk, maca, and peppermint extract, then pour into a mug.

Sunrise Nojito (MOCKTAIL)

A satiating and savory affair of the senses, this anti-inflammatory mocktail is awesome for any occasion. It has a vibrant orange color, a refreshing herbal bouquet, and just enough lemon juice to take the edge off the carrot juice's sweet nature. Sage is used to improve cognitive abilities, specifically in people with Alzheimer's, and to lower blood sugar and cholesterol. Fresh turmeric is now more available, and I have found the root to be much more effective for alleviating inflammation and inflammation-based pain. The taste is mild, but it can still take some getting used to, so if you aren't in the habit of using the fresh root yet, you can always start with less.

15 fresh mint leaves

6 fresh sage leaves

1 teaspoon grated turmeric

½ ounce fresh lemon juice

7 ounces carrot juice

Muddle the mint, sage, and turmeric with the lemon juice in a shaker.

Add ice and the carrot juice, then shake.

Pour directly into a highball glass.

Kava Chameleon

(MOCKTAIL)

Kava is a slightly intoxicating herb that needs some major loving assistance when it comes to helping its dirtlike flavor taste a bit more palatable. Mint does the trick, as it soothes any potential nausea the kava might cause, especially to first-time drinkers. Kava is known for its "reverse tolerance" effect, which means that you might need to drink it several times before you feel it. You can also get different effects out of different types, so when purchasing kava, go with the description (sedating, social, et cetera) that best matches what you're looking for.

12 fresh mint leaves

½ dropperful toffee stevia

2 ounces prepared kava liquid (follow the directions on the package)

Muddle the mint with the toffee stevia in a shaker.

Add the kava and shake with ice, then strain into a shot glass.

 THINKING Girl's NOTE

Start slow when drinking kava, but if you feel nothing after an hour or two, don't be afraid to go back for another.

A Walk
IN THE
Flowers

If there's one weird thing in life I'm a fan of (and to be honest, I'm a fan of a ton of weird things), it's eating flowers. The idea that something so beautiful can be consumed, which is then processed by our physical bodies and used for fuel, is just a crazy magical concept to me. Because I enjoy eating flowers, it's a natural migration to love the act of drinking them too.

Floral flavors are more mainstream than many people realize, though they are more commonly used in other cultures than in the United States. You may have noticed that we've already used them a bunch in this book because they contribute fabulously to an array of cocktail and mocktail recipes!

In this chapter, the focus is on fresh flowers, floral teas, flower liqueurs, and flower waters. Their health benefits are as varied as their tastes; for example, rose is heavily perfumed and used for calming, hibiscus is sour and aids in weight loss, and marigold, known in the medicine world as calendula, is mild and promotes healing. Be sure to only use flowers that are *clearly* denoted as edible, which all the ones in these recipes are; anything else could make you sick. And now, let's take a walk in the flowers and make some delicious drinks!

Marigold Pleasure

Orange and glowing like a floral cocktail sunset, the marigolds in this drink contribute more to its beauty than to its flavor—but it's so gorgeous that no one should mind that! As mentioned, marigolds are light in taste, which is a reason they are commonly added to salad green mixes; unlike bitter nasturtiums, another common salad additive, they don't upset the status quo of your salad or your drink. I encourage you to sip the flowers right on up your straw for their anti-inflammatory and wound-healing properties! Tropical with orgeat syrup and tart with lemon, this is a bourbon cocktail to woo a crowd.

Petals of 2 marigolds

¾ ounce fresh lemon juice

2 ounces bourbon

¾ ounce orgeat syrup (page 248)

1 whole marigold flower top, for garnish

Muddle the marigold petals with the lemon juice in a shaker.

Add ice and the remaining ingredients (except the garnish) and shake.

Pour directly into a highball glass. Garnish with the marigold flower top.

Light as a Lily

Jasmine tea is reminiscent of fresh jasmine flowers with its heady nose, so I recommend brewing it with just a small amount of water to pack the most punch of floral love possible into this cocktail. Jasmine tea is typically composed of jasmine flowers brewed with green tea, so you get the antioxidant catechins of the tea alongside the mood-lifting and nerve-calming effects of the flower. Elderflower liqueur provides just enough added sweetness, and thankfully elderflowers themselves lower blood sugar, so the liqueur cancels itself out a bit! Elderflower is also helpful for respiratory issues and is antiseptic enough to be used as a mouthwash. I don't suggest gargling with this cocktail, but it's nice to know that as you sip it you're getting some kindness from the flowers you're consuming!

Petals of 2 edible flowers (such as pansy or nasturtium)

2 ounces strongly brewed jasmine tea

2 ounces American/New Western gin

½ ounce fresh lemon juice

½ ounce elderflower liqueur

Muddle the flower petals with the tea in a shaker.

Add the remaining ingredients and ice, then shake.

Pour directly into a Collins glass.

We Met in the Garden

This cocktail is distinctly tart, with floral flavors of both hibiscus and rose. With rose water, a little dash will do you; it's incredibly potent and a small, inexpensive bottle will last quite a long time even with regular usage. Known as a symbol of love throughout the ages, roses are uplifting and aphrodisiac in nature. They're also very healthful, as they are antiseptic and great for stomach issues. Hibiscus is excellent for the liver, making this gin-based beverage just a touch less serious than it would otherwise be. London Dry gin was our choice here for its dryness, which picks up the flavors of rose and hibiscus, and its juniper quality melds well with them.

2 ounces London Dry gin

½ ounce fresh lime juice

½ ounce hibiscus liqueur

1 dash rose water

1 lime wheel, for garnish

Shake all the ingredients (except the garnish) in a shaker with ice.

Strain into a champagne saucer and garnish with the lime wheel.

Until the Bitter End

A cocktail as bitter as We Met in the Garden (opposite) is sour, this is another adult beverage for those who enjoy adult flavors over syrupy-sweet ones. The artichoke leaf liqueur Cynar provides just enough sweetness to work with the other ingredients, such as potent orange blossom water. Even stronger than rose water, orange blossom water adds a floral citrus taste and aroma. It's a by-product of bitter orange essential-oil production, and is used to ease stomach upset, lower cholesterol, and soothe a sore throat or cough. The herb bitters brings the cocktail together to give it the distinct feature of wildflowers in a forest.

1½ ounces vodka

1½ ounces Cynar

1 dash orange blossom water

1 dash Swedish herb bitters

Stir all the ingredients in a mixing glass with ice.

Strain into a rocks glass and serve .

Orange You Glad

Initially, I tried to avoid the use of amaretto in this book, as I've always considered it a cloyingly sweet, cheap liqueur. Little did I know that you can buy natural versions of it that are positively scrumptious! The amarettos that Brittini introduced me to had me wondering how I've been living without that nutty bite for all this time; they are free of additives, artificial flavorings, and everything else we'd rather keep out of this book and our bellies. Orange blossom water adds to the coastal, beachy feel, and scotch keeps us close to the shore with earthy aromas.

1½ ounces scotch

½ ounce amaretto

1 dash orange blossom water

Stir all the ingredients in a mixing glass with ice, then strain into a rocks glass with a single large ice cube.

Flower Shooter

Tequila shot time!!! Even better, these tequila shots basically taste like flowers. If you aren't a huge fan of tequila's flavor, this shot will be your new bestie. Lavender syrup sweetens the deal without any added sugar, and rose water cuts right through tequila's odd aroma, balancing it out with good, loving vibes. A touch of lime juice is, of course, the natural match to tequila; since it's included in the shot, there's no need to go biting down on a wedge after you drink it.

1 ounce tequila

¾ ounce lavender syrup (page 248)

¼ ounce fresh lime juice

1 dash rose water

Shake all the ingredients in a shaker with ice.

Strain into a double shot glass.

THINKING
Girl's
NOTE

If you still want to lick salt off your hands you can, but with how yummy this shot tastes you likely won't feel the need to.

Luscious Lavender

(MOCKTAIL)

There are no calories in this mocktail, as it's a superbly simple soda of sugarless lavender syrup and sparkling mineral water. Lavender is a scent that nearly everyone loves, and luckily it also has a strong uplifting effect on mood as well as providing pain relief for cuts and burns! I make my own burn cream and tattoo salve, and neither would be a fraction as effective without the lavender. Here, you can both taste and reap the benefits of lavender, all without any guilt about the fact that you're drinking a sweet bubbly beverage.

1½ ounces lavender syrup (page 248)

Sparkling mineral water, to fill

Fill a mason jar with ice and add the lavender syrup.

Add the sparkling water to top and stir gently.

Love
Shots (MOCKTAIL)

Looking for love in all the right places? You must be, because you found this simple and amorous mocktail! A quick and easy blend of hibiscus tea and rose water, this mocktail is a vibrant red that tastes every bit as luscious as it looks. Hibiscus is a tart tea, used to speed up metabolism and assist with liver issues. Rose water is sweet in its bouquet on the nose but not on the taste buds, so this drink won't overpower you with the candy flavor it looks like it may possess. I love it as an aperitif before a meal, in lieu of dessert to end a meal, or as part of a romantic night in. Give yourself an extra shot at romance with this sultry little shot of love!

4 ounces brewed hibiscus tea, chilled

2 dashes rose water

Add the tea and rose water to a double shot glass and stir.

On the one hand, we're all grown-ups here and Jell-O shots are ridiculously juvenile. On the other hand, I still shop in the juniors department and I just got my nineteenth tattoo, so hey, *whatever*. Also known as solid cocktails, cocktail gelées, jelly shots, edible cocktails, and gelled cocktails, these babies are a good time waiting to happen! Jell-O shots are as fun as anything could possibly be, they're delicious, and grass-fed gelatin is legitimately very healthy.

In an alcohol-specific sense, the protein content slows down the absorption of the alcohol into your bloodstream, effectively rationing your buzz for you. In a wider sense, grass-fed gelatin is anti-inflammatory, gut healing, helps you recover from bone, joint, or cartilage injuries, and is excellent for immunity. To "bloom" your gelatin, simply follow the instructions on the gelatin package, and if "blooming" gelatin sounds daunting, all it means is that you need to sprinkle gelatin over liquid and let it sit.

Feeling left out because you and/or your friends are vegan? I have you covered too! In any recipe that calls for gelatin, simply omit it. Instead, substitute an equal amount of agar-agar powder and boil it with the liquid you'd otherwise add the gelatin to for ten minutes, or until the agar-agar is fully dissolved and somewhat thickened. If you have agar-agar flakes instead of powder, use double the quantity of gelatin that is called for.

Cookies 'n' Crème Pudding

Yes, I said pudding . . . and I mean it! This edible cocktail is dangerous, and by dangerous I mean dangerously delicious—but don't go eating a vat of it! It's pretty low in alcohol, making it a reasonable dessert that won't get anyone too buzzed unless he or she does actually eat a vat of it. The vanilla bean provides the perfect cookies-and-cream visual effect while also contributing trace minerals and B vitamins. Coconut products are antifungal, helping to undo some of the effects of the liqueur. This was one cocktail that we just couldn't stop tasting as we went along!

1 tablespoon gelatin

5 ounces coconut milk

Scrapings from 1 inch of a vanilla bean

2 ounces clear crème de cacao

Bloom the gelatin in the coconut milk for 5 minutes.

Heat the coconut milk and gelatin mixture in a small pot over low heat until thoroughly dissolved, 3 to 5 minutes.

Remove from the heat, stir in the vanilla bean scrapings and the crème de cacao, and pour into molds or a small pan.

Chill until firm, at least 2 hours.

THINKING Girl's NOTE

I recommend portioning this into individual cups or molds, as trusting yourself or others to take a scoop and leave the rest is risky business!

Crushed Crimson

To juice a watermelon yourself, simply place the chunks in a blender and blend, then strain through a sieve. If you'd like additional health value, include the white part of the rind! That's where many different vitamins are. The fruit flesh itself is high in lycopene, and unlike tomatoes, your body can process the raw watermelon lycopene well, and the rind contains citrulline. Citrulline is an amino acid that can be used to help treat male erectile dysfunction and to boost athletic performance. Hibiscus liqueur and rum turn this into a true summer affair, vivacious in color and youthful in flavor. White rum is the best choice for this drink because the watermelon can be easily overpowered by alcohol with a darker rum.

1 tablespoon gelatin

4 ounces fresh watermelon juice

1 ounce white rum

1 ounce hibiscus liqueur

Bloom the gelatin in the watermelon juice for 5 minutes.

Heat the juice and gelatin mixture in a small pot over low heat until thoroughly dissolved, 3 to 5 minutes.

Remove from the heat, add the rum and liqueur, and pour into molds or a small pan.

Chill until firm, at least 2 hours.

Red Snapper Gelée

From Sorority Girls (page 242) to an offshoot of a Bloody Mary cocktail that is decidedly at least thirty-something, we're covering everyone's gelled cocktail tastes here! When you make a Bloody Mary with gin, it becomes a red snapper; when you make it with gelatin, it becomes a heavenly gelée that can be eaten with a spoon and would make an amazing party appetizer, especially if served like a soup shot. Coconut aminos take the place of Worcestershire sauce as a healthful alternative with multiple essential amino acids and no MSG. They have a similar umami character without any of the headache potential, making them a perfect swap for this cocktail and beyond (I'm talking to you, steak!).

1 tablespoon gelatin

4 ounces tomato juice

1 ounce gin

½ ounce fresh lemon juice

2 dashes coconut aminos

1 pinch horseradish

1 pinch cracked black pepper

Bloom the gelatin in the tomato juice for 5 minutes.

Heat the tomato juice and gelatin mixture in a small pot over low heat until thoroughly dissolved, 3 to 5 minutes.

Remove from the heat, add the remaining ingredients, and pour into molds or a small pan.

Chill until firm, at least 2 hours.

Ruby Red Lipstick

As perfect as tawny port was for Any Port in a Storm (page 191), ruby port goes equally well in this gelled shot. The flavor and color of it paired with pomegranate juice is absolutely perfect, and it's just boozy enough to give you a slight buzz without any hard alcohol. Pomegranate has been controversial for its purported benefits versus its actual ones, and since the POM juice company is owned by people with my same last name, I'm hesitant to speak too much to that lest they ever want to include me in the distant-family empire! I will say with certainty that the fruit has potent antioxidants, higher than green tea, cranberries, or blueberries. And I will say that paired with ruby port, if it were lipstick it would be a lipstick color you'd want to wear endlessly.

1 tablespoon gelatin

4 ounces pomegranate juice

3 ounces ruby port

Bloom the gelatin in the pomegranate juice for 5 minutes.

Heat the juice and gelatin mixture in a small pot over low heat until thoroughly dissolved, 3 to 5 minutes.

Remove from the heat, add the port, and pour into molds or a small pan.

Chill until firm, at least 2 hours.

Sorority Girls

Pineapple juice and vodka is the most "basic" youthful cocktail we can think of. While I generally suggest fresh juice wherever possible, with pineapple you want to be sure to use a pasteurized product because the enzymes in the raw stuff will prevent gelling! Since pineapple juice contains bromelain, an anti-inflammatory enzyme that is also good for digestion, this is a good choice if you're liquoring up not too long after dinner. Bright sunshine yellow in color and mellowy fruity in taste, this is a gel cocktail that practically anyone would be happy cozying up next to.

1 tablespoon gelatin

5 ounces pineapple juice

2 ounces vodka

Bloom the gelatin in the pineapple juice for 5 minutes.

Heat the juice and gelatin in a small pot over low heat until thoroughly dissolved, 3 to 5 minutes.

Remove from the heat, add the vodka, and pour into molds or a small pan.

Chill until firm, at least 2 hours.

We Stayed in the Garden

In the flower chapter We Met in the Garden (page 224), and, well, things went nicely enough that I thought we might like to stay there a while, so I solidified the cocktail! Because booze becomes more prominent in gelled form than in a liquid cocktail, we reduced the gin content down to an ounce for our purpose here. Fear not, it's still plenty intoxicating, since we kept the hibiscus liqueur quantity. Just like its liquid counterpart, this gelatin shot will please your palate with multiple angles of floral notes! Rose water loses some of its strength in this setting, so be sure to use the full two dashes in order to taste it.

1 tablespoon gelatin

2 ounces fresh lime juice

2 dashes rose water

1 ounce London Dry gin

2 ounces hibiscus liqueur

Bloom the gelatin in the lime juice and rose water for 5 minutes.

Heat the juice and gelatin mixture in a small pot over low heat until thoroughly dissolved, 3 to 5 minutes.

Remove from the heat, add the gin and liqueur, and pour into molds or a small pan.

Chill until firm, at least 2 hours.

Fruit Cup

(MOCKTAIL)

Did I ever get fruit cups growing up? Not so much. There was plenty of fruit, but it rarely came in plastic. Instead, for a similar treat my mom would blend fruit and then gel it with agar-agar. It was like the fruit cups that other kids had, at least kind of. I still love blended fruit gelatin, and we add just enough juice here to give it a standard gelatin-dessert texture. This is a great option to serve in small containers to guests who want to partake in fun but not booze, or to keep a batch on hand for yourself when you want a little treat without the alcohol.

1 tablespoon gelatin

3 ounces fresh orange juice

1 cup fresh or frozen peaches, blended

Bloom the gelatin in the orange juice for several minutes.

Heat the juice and gelatin mixture in a small pot over low heat until thoroughly dissolved, 3 to 5 minutes.

Remove from the heat, add the blended peaches, and pour into molds or a small pan.

Chill until firm, at least 2 hours.

Grape Happy (MOCKTAIL)

If you were brought up in a more mainstream home than I was, your grape gelatin dessert may not have contained any grape products at all. Oddly enough, grape juice and agar-agar (aka kanten or hippie Jell-O) tastes surprisingly similar to that version—just less sweet. No matter what you were served for a purple treat, this jelly mocktail will take you back to those good old days. Grape kombucha gets mellowed down here in flavor by way of gelatin and firmed up into a treat you can serve the same way you'd serve an alcoholic jelly shot.

1 tablespoon gelatin

6 ounces grape kombucha

Bloom the gelatin in the kombucha for 5 minutes; note that it may bubble up a bit.

Heat the kombucha and gelatin mixture in a small pot over low heat until thoroughly dissolved, 3 to 5 minutes.

Remove from the heat and pour into molds or a small pan.

Chill until firm, at least 2 hours.

I recommend GT Dave's grape flavor, since it is made with Concord grapes and has the most childhoodlike taste.

THINKING Girl's NOTE

Cheer Up Syrups

These four easy-to-make syrups are used throughout this book to flavor many of our drinks. I created them in the hopes that they'd help you add fun to your bevvies without feeling the need to reach for any actual white sugar.

I used coconut sugar, honey, and maple syrup for caloric sweeteners, and Swerve erythritol for noncaloric. While Swerve is erythritol based, note that it's the FOS prebiotic ingredient in it that prevents it from seizing; the lavender syrup would not be possible if attempted with a straight erythritol powder. All the syrups are pared-down versions of classics that generally take much longer to prepare, as I wanted you to *actually* make them!

They'll keep in the fridge for at least a week or two, and so can be used on more than one occasion; if you're concerned about waste and know you won't be using them repeatedly, recipes can be halved or quartered without issue. As for the food ingredients, like sliced ginger or vanilla bean, I choose to keep them in the final product to keep the flavor going, but you can strain them if you prefer.

Sugarless Lavender Syrup

1½ cups room-temperature filtered water

½ cup Swerve sweetener

1 large sprig lavender, or more to taste

Bring all the ingredients to a boil in a saucepan, then remove from the heat and cool.

Orgeat Syrup

½ cup honey (substitute maple syrup if vegan)

½ cup hot water

1 tablespoon almond extract

½ teaspoon orange blossom water

½ teaspoon rose water

Mix all the ingredients together until the honey (or maple syrup) is thoroughly dissolved.

Vanilla Syrup

1 cup room-temperature filtered water

½ cup coconut sugar

½ cup honey (substitute maple syrup if vegan)

2 teaspoons vanilla extract

Scrapings of 1 vanilla bean

Bring all the ingredients to a boil in a saucepan, then remove from the heat and cool.

Ginger Syrup

1 cup room-temperature filtered water

½ cup coconut sugar

½ cup maple syrup

4 ¼-inch-thick ginger slices

Bring all the ingredients to a boil in a saucepan, then remove from the heat and cool.

Spirits Glossary

Absinthe: A noticeably herbal spirit, absinthe was banned in the United States in 1912 in part because a key ingredient, wormwood, was thought to be toxic in large doses. In 2007, scientists concluded that modern bottlings are safe—and luckily for us it is absolutely delicious in cocktails!

Amaretto: Sweet and bitter almonds, apricot pits, and vanilla comprise this liqueur that saw its beginnings in Italy. Even though Disaronno looks delicious on television, Luxardo Amaretto contains less sugar and has a much more robust flavor.

Aquavit: Produced since the fifteenth century, it is primarily a Scandinavian liquor that derives its unique flavor from caraway seeds, star anise, dill, or fennel. Aquavit is the perfect substitute to vodka or gin in a cocktail when you are looking for an earthy character or viscous texture. We prefer Linie Aquavit, not only for its superior flavor, but because it also crosses the equator twice before it's bottled, and no, it doesn't need a passport!

Benedictine: A French amber-colored herbal liqueur designed by Benedictine monks utilizing a recipe they have kept secret since 1510. It's composed of hyssop, angelica, and lemon balm.

Bitters: Now a very broad term, bitters pertains to all bitter liqueurs and, well, bitters. They are made from herb and root extracts as well as spices, predominantly from the calming components of tropical and subtropical plants. Originally created and sold as "patent medicines," these unique tinctures have found their home alongside aperitifs and digestifs. Bitters are widely used to increase a cocktail's complexity by adding flavor and balancing ingredients. Here, we use a variety of flavors and brands of bitters; hell, there is even a chapter dedicated to the category!

Bourbon: An American grain spirit comprised of at least 51% corn and aged in brand-new charred American oak barrels for a minimum of two years. We enjoyed working with bottles from Four Roses and Buffalo Trace, because they use non-GMO corn in all their whiskeys. Generally it is thought that the gluten content is distilled out of the mashes, but if you are particularly sensitive to gluten, exercise caution when trying bourbon or just avoid it.

Brandy: A category just as broad as whiskey, brandy can be literally anything distilled from fermented fruit juice. Cognac is one of the most well-known examples, but here we experiment with Spanish brandy. Brandy de Jerez exemplifies the best of Spanish brandy; it must be aged in used sherry barrels in the district of Andalusia, allowing for full and complex flavors.

Byrrh: A French aperitif that originated in the nineteenth century, it consists of unfermented grape juice (mistelle), wine, botanicals, and spices that are aged in oak barrels. It's similar to sweet vermouth but with added notes of strawberry and bitter quinine. If you're in doubt of how to pronounce it, just say "beer."

Cacao: A liqueur traditionally produced with cocoa beans, it may be clear or a dark caramel color. Tempus Fugit Spirits has a tasty crème de cacao that is completely natural in color and free of added caramel.

Campari: An Italian aperitif that is bitter orange in flavor and red in color. This particular spirit tends to be an acquired taste, so if you have not encountered it before, you might want to purchase one of the smaller bottles. Leopold Apertivo, the first American take on this classic bitters, is a 100% all-natural substitution for Campari.

Chartreuse: Bottles that probably contain the most unique stories in spirit history, Chartreuse has been produced by the Carthusian monks (yes, monks!) from France since 1605, and only three people know the actual recipe. A blend of about 130 unrevealed plants comprise these green and yellow distillates, which are so unique in flavor that most imitations have failed. Imagine sweet, herbal, citrus, and earthy all in one—but better.

Cognac: A brandy (see also "Brandy") from the Cognac region of France. When buying for the house, we prefer to skip the V.S. and go straight for the V.S.O.P., where the youngest brandy in the bottle has been aged for a minimum of at least four years, versus only two in the V.S. category.

Cointreau: The original top-shelf curaçao orange liqueur from France that helped drinks such as the Margarita, Sidecar, and Cosmopolitan become the cocktail icons they are today. But buyer beware: Don't be fooled by cheap imitations.

Crème de Cacao: See "Cacao."

Crème Yvette: An American-born violet liqueur with berries, vanilla, and spices.

Cynar: A bitter Italian liqueur that has artichoke as the star ingredient alongside dark cocoa and spice. Also categorized as an amaro.

Cynar 70: The higher-proofed sibling to Cynar, Cynar 70 comes in at 35% alcohol by volume.

Damiana: The national spirit of Mexico, it is a liqueur made from the plant of the same name. This indigenous herb of Baja, California, is rumored to be an aphrodisiac and improves fertility.

Elderflower liqueur: Exactly what you think it is—a liqueur made from elderflower! Although there is nothing wrong with the traditional St. Germain (aka ketchup for cocktails), we enjoy working with Thatcher's Elderflower, which utilizes all-natural, sustainably farmed, organic ingredients.

Falernum: A syrup or liqueur that was developed in the West Indies, utilizing ingredients such as ginger, clove, almond, and lime. We choose the alcoholic version for our drinks.

Fernet: A bitter Italian amaro made with various herbs and spices (most notably saffron). There are a growing number of fernets on the market; for our purposes we recommend the easy sipper and pocket-friendly R. Jelinek fernet.

Gin: A neutral grain spirit that is traditionally flavored with various botanicals, herbs, and spices, including citrus peels, coriander, cassia, anise, angelica root, cardamom, and, most important, juniper berry. It has embodied different adaptations since its conception by the Dutch in the 1600s. Today, the most popular is the London Dry style. For our purposes, we chose The Botanist gin from Scotland for our London Dry, due to its quality and flavor. Another style that is increasing in popularity is the New Western style of gin; Junipero from San Francisco is an excellent choice. As with many other spirits, choosing a quality gin is extremely important, if not mandatory! Otherwise, you will be the victim of a severe hangover.

Leopold Bros. Three Pins Alpine Herbal Liqueur: By far one of the most unique spirits in this book (and a personal favorite), Three Pins Alpine Herbal Liqueur is a blend of fifteen herbs and flowers from the Rocky Mountain region of the United States that have been hand-selected. Some of the proprietary herbs include gingko biloba, echinacea, coriander, and orange zest. Please be sure to refrigerate it after opening.

Mezcal: The parent category to tequila, mezcal is primarily produced in Oaxaca, Mexico, and made from multiple types of agave plants. When making mezcal (or mescal), the piña of the agave plant is slow-roasted underground with hot stones, giving mezcal a much smokier and earthy flavor in comparison to tequila.

Pedro Ximénez: Pedro Ximénez (or "PX," as it is commonly referred to) is quite a distinct and unique distillate. It resides in the sherry family, but its initial flavor profile would suggest otherwise; sporting a dark chestnut color, PX is rich, sweet, and velvety on the palate with complex flavors of caramel, figs, nuts, spices, and dried fruits. Do yourself a favor and buy a bottle! Both abstainers of dessert and sweet fanatics alike will enjoy a dram tremendously.

Port: A dessert wine from Portugal. Tawny ports are nuttier, drier, and generally preferable to ruby ports. Please be aware that port is a form of wine, so it does have a shelf life.

Rum: Said to be the first spirit of the New World, having been produced in Barbados and Jamaica in the mid-seventeenth century. This overly delicious yet underrated spirit is made from molasses and sugarcane juice or syrup. Various spices can be added to create the popular spiced rum. We favor California native Crusoe Organic Spiced Rum as well as the Chairman's Reserve Spiced.

Sambuca: An Italian after-dinner liqueur that is anise-based and has a licorice flavor, typically due to the use of the elderberry bush.

Scotch: Quite simply, a word for whiskey produced in Scotland that has been aged for a minimum of three years. We used two different styles of scotch whisky: single malt and blended. Single malt scotch comes from a single distillery and is always made from 100% malted barley. Blended scotch is a combination of those single malt whiskies as well as grain spirits. For those of you who are looking for a scotch alternative, Nikka Coffee Grain from Japan has a similar effect in cocktails and is 97% corn.

Soju: A distilled Japanese spirit that is traditionally produced from rice, wheat, or barley. On a rare occasion you can find soju produced from other starches, such as potatoes, sweet potatoes, and tapioca.

Sparkling wine: A style of wine bottled with carbon dioxide either by fermentation or injection, the result is bubbly and is commonly drunk during celebrations. We use styles such as champagne (from France) and drier styles like cava and prosecco.

Spiced Rum: See "Rum."

Tequila: Oh, tequila, a spirit that can simultaneously give you one of the best and worst drinking experiences of your life (according to Brittini's mother, anyway). Tequila is a beverage distilled from the blue agave plant that results in one of the most complex and exciting spirits. The majority of tequilas can be categorized as *blanco* or *plata* (bottled within sixty days of distillation), *reposado* or *rested* (aged two to eleven months in oak), and *anejo* (aged for one year or more in oak barrels). Due to high demand and overproduction, most tequilas have lost their quality (Patrón, anyone?). For our purposes we love working with Forteleza and Siete Leguas, who maintain their original production practices. (Fun fact: Even though most people think the agave plant is similar to a cactus, it is actually a member of the lily family.)

Vermouth: Traditionally, Italian or French fortified wine flavored with various botanicals. There are multiple styles, the most produced being categorized as sweet or dry. Our palates keep bringing us back to Carpano Antica for our sweet and Dolin Dry, for our, well, dry.

Vodka: A neutral spirit distilled from almost anything and found anywhere in the world. Its sole purpose is to have little to no flavor (small, craft distilleries excluded). We prefer U.S. natives Boyd & Blair's Potato Vodka, expertly crafted using only locally sourced potatoes or Sonoma Valley's grape-based Hanson vodka, certified organic and gluten-free.

Resources

Rest assured that no matter how uncommon an ingredient in this book may sound, all are easily available online, if not in person! The following are my suggestions for where to source the less-usual ingredients if they are not readily available at your local grocery or health store.

Food-grade essential oils: There are many brands (such as DoTerra and Young Living) that make great quality organic and edible essential oils. Personally, I tend to eschew direct-buying companies and prefer easy websites, so I recommend Mountain Rose Herbs for their quality, economic value, and ease of ordering. You can purchase any oils used in this book at MountainRoseHerbs.com.

Grass-fed collagen: I prefer the brand from BULLETPROOF® Coffee, as I find it's the easiest to dissolve. It's available at Bulletproof.com or on Amazon.

Grass-fed gelatin: Sadly, I've never seen this in a single store, not even the largest Whole Foods! Both Great Lakes and Vital Proteins are of excellent quality and available on Amazon. Just be sure to order the gelatin, not the collagen peptides, for gelling.

Kava: I experimented with multiple styles and preparations of kava, and found that even as a person who is fine with high-maintenance foods, the noninstant kavas were too much of a pain for me. I suggest the instant type that can be blended into a drink over the powder that needs a ten-minute massage (no joke, it does!). All forms are available online and on Amazon. Note that I don't recommend getting kava with ingredients added, or it will affect the taste of the kava cocktail recipes in this book.

Maca Bliss powder and He Shou Wu: As indicated in the recipes, my favorite brand for these is Longevity Power because they are much more digestible than other brands. They can be purchased at LongevityPower.com.

MCT Oil: This is another product where I use BULLETPROOF® Coffee, and favor their Brain Octane oil over the XCT oil because it is more concentrated in bacteria-fighting caprylic acid. You can purchase it on Amazon or at Bulletproof.com.

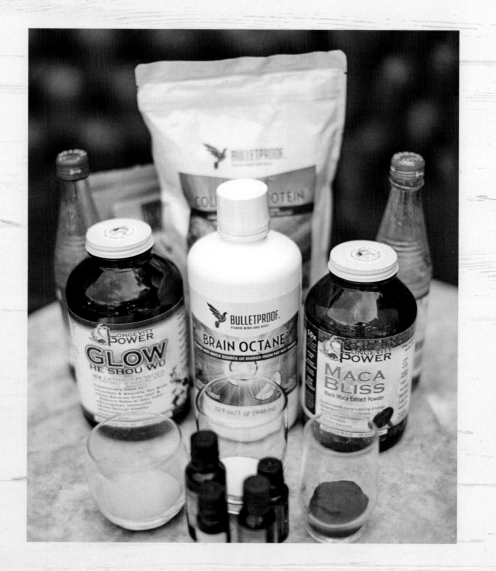

Acknowledgments

The *Thinking Girl's Guide to Drinking* was made possible by a whole slew of thinking girls as well as a few thinking guys. For everyone who played a part in making this project come together, my thanks and gratitude! The universe has once again shown me that as long as I follow my path and maintain that good old attitude of gratitude, life will be an ever-evolving dream.

Brittini Rae, my contributor: I couldn't have found a more qualified, knowledgeable, invested partner. This would not have been possible without you, and I'm so thrilled we were able to share the journey together!

Coleen O'Shea, my superstar literary agent, who helped me suss out the concept, matched my speed, and supported me all along the way.

Sheila Conlin, my manager, who continues to build me in more ways than I can measure.

My editor, Jordana Tusman, who blew me away with edits that I'd swear came back faster than I could send her copy, and Breanne Sommer for her excellent PR work.

Leela Cyd and her stylist Ayda Robana, and Maggie Davis and Vanessa Smith for their beautiful photography.

Richard Ljoenes and Laura Klynstra for turning that photography and my writing into this work of art.

Judith Regan, who had me convinced within five minutes of conversation that I would never be satisfied with any other publisher.

Sat Devbir Singh, my Kundalini teacher and healer, who clears all blocks along this path with his magic.

My mother, father, and sister, who are always there for me and always teaching me something.

Houston Hospitality for the usage of No Vacancy.

Chanty, the best-looking man in the world, and Lala, the most unusually plush woman.

You, dear wonderful person who cared enough about your own happiness and health to read a healthier cocktails and mocktails book. You are why I'm here.

Index

Note: Page numbers in italics indicate photographs.